This book is a gift to you from Scottish Book Trust, a
national charity changing lives through reading and
writing, to celebrate Book Week Scotland
(14–20 November 2022) and Scotland's Year
of Stories 2022.

bookweekscotland.com

Scotland's Stories is a collection of true stories written
by the people of Scotland. This book is one of
70,000 **free** copies – thank you for picking it up!
If you enjoy it, help us share it with as many people
as possible. Dip into it and share a few favourites
with friends, display it, gift a copy to a partner,
colleague or parent, or even leave it somewhere
for a stranger to discover.
(We recommend a reading age of 15+.)

These stories are both funny and moving, paying
tribute to the breadth of storytelling across multiple
generations all over Scotland. If you enjoy this book,
please consider making a donation so that everyone
in Scotland has the opportunity to improve their life
chances through books and the fundamental skills of
reading and writing.

Visit **scottishbooktrust.com/donate** to find out
more.

Happy reading!
#BookWeekScotland

A huge thank you to the following individuals who supported Scottish Book Trust as members of The Book Club

Gordon Dalyell and Pamela Leslie

Marian and Mark Deere

Martin Adam and William Zachs

Robert Hill

Scott Lothian

and those who wish to remain anonymous

Scotland's Stories

scottishbooktrust.com

First published in 2022 by Scottish Book Trust,
Sandeman House, Trunk's Close, 55 High Street,
Edinburgh EH1 1SR

scottishbooktrust.com

The authors' right to be identified as an author of this book under
the Copyright, Patents and Designs Act 1988 has been asserted

A CIP catalogue record for this book is available
from the British Library

Typeset by Laura Jones

Printed and bound by CPI Group (UK) Ltd, Croydon CR0 4YY

Scottish Book Trust makes every effort to ensure that the paper
used in this book has been legally sourced from well-
managed and sustainable forests

Cover design by Craig Laurenson

This is a free book, designed to be read alone or in groups, enjoyed,
shared and passed on to friends. This book is gifted to you by
Scottish Book Trust for Book Week Scotland 2022

Digital editions of this book are available from
scottishbooktrust.com

Contents

Community legends

Everybody's Auntie, by Angela McKenna   2

Egg and Chips, by Sarah Houston   6

In a While, Crocodile, by Laura Law   9

Blue Car, by CE Ayr   13

An t-Òban, by Angus Peter Campbell*   18

Machaire Na Hearadh: A' Fàs is A' Dol Fàs,
    by Mòrag Anna NicNèill*   20

Making it home

The Seeds of Our Home,
    by Diana Monteiro Toombs   28

Pakistani Life in 1960s Glasgow, by Lubna Kerr   32

Spellbound, by Sue Palmer   36

On a Sense of (s)p(l)ace, by Raman Mundair*   39

Walls, by Margaret Grant   43

Origin stories

Because Ah Matter, by Angel Rodgers   46

Epona, by Elizabeth Craig   51

Dear, by ED Robertson   53

Inspired by Ladybirds, by Linda Brown   56

The Berries, by Angela Logan   60

Something Precious?, by Vivien Jones   64

The Jakit, Mysticism n PPK Resurrection,
    by Graeme Armstrong*   68

Finding my place

A Ceilidh Through Time, by Jacqueline Munro   74

Here, by Fiona Stuart   77

Clachnaben, by Jane Swanson   80

Sunday. . . (Black and White), by Des Mcanulty   83

Let the Shadows Fall, by Helen Fields*   85

Tales to treasure

Foxes, by Iris Potter   90

She's Got the Beat, by Paul Foy   92

Cheesie McCraw, by Jennie Murray   96

The Quilted Dressing Gown,
    by Hannah McDonald   98

Faeries, by Jamie Aitken   102

Yellowcraig, by Kirsty Niven   106

*Stories by published authors.
Please be aware that this book is unsuitable for readers aged 14 or younger as it contains strong language and mature content.

Community legends

Everybody's Auntie
Angela McKenna

The mid-sixties was a time when your mammy's pals were called your aunties, and nobody bothered. I had armfuls of them, aunties, and I had an extra granny, an elderly woman who lived across the road and who found me quite entertaining for such a wee thing. My memories of her are vague, and I don't know if she was anybody's real granny, but I do remember she was kind to me and that I liked her.

As for the auntie situation, it never occurred to me to question how I could have so many of them, even when I discovered that my Auntie Agnes seemed to be everybody's auntie. I called her auntie, and so did my mother and the extended family. In fact, everybody called her auntie, except for my granny, whose auntie she actually was; she just called her Agnes, which I always thought was quite daring.

Agnes was born in 1907 to a poor family. Of the many children born to her mother, Mary, only Agnes and one sister survived to adulthood, the rest dying in infancy – apart from one girl who died of consumption as a young teenager. It was a hard life, made all the more challenging by the head of the household, Auld Tam, a miner and a drunken brute whose reputation for ferocious violence was such that even the local polis kept their distance.

Although Auld Tam terrorised the community, one person in the district didn't fear him: Agnes. It was an oft-told tale that one day years later, when only Agnes and Auld Tam lived in their room and kitchen, she came home at lunchtime from her job as a weaver to find her father inebriated and roaring in anger as usual. When she refused to make him anything to eat because it would make her late for work, he grabbed that day's newspaper, set it ablaze, and threw it onto the bed in the big room. Agnes just looked at him, then turned her back and told him to burn what he fancied. She then left for work as the brute fought the flames on his own. When telling this story, my granny always added that Agnes stayed in the house with Auld Tam until he died. Not out of love or duty but because she had been too fussy when it came to men and had 'watched the hats 'til the bunnets went by'. Perhaps that's true; I can't be sure. I wonder, though, whether her antipathy towards the blissful state of matrimony didn't have its roots in what she saw around her: drunken, violent men ruling over women who worked inside and outside the home and who were nothing more than skivvies. I think Agnes might have looked at the hats and the bunnets and found no significant difference between them. And so it was that she settled into the single life surrounded by good pals.

Naturally, the single life had many plus points, not least the absence of hungry weans and a husband drinking and gambling his way through the weekly wages. So, Agnes lived comfortably, unlike most of her family and friends who struggled to make ends meet and for whom the pawnshop was a regular haunt. It was always said, though, that Agnes was good to people; she would never see anyone go hungry or any wean shoeless. I can vouch for both. Nary a Sunday passed when Agnes didn't arrive, straight from the chapel via a detour to the Barras, laden with something for everyone. If I was lucky, she'd bring me a wee bag of puff candy or maybe a bagatelle, its cardboard backing musty and soft from sitting too long on the stall. If I was unlucky, she'd bring me a jumper!

It wasn't until I was well into my teens that I understood how Agnes's largesse was the difference between survival and the breadline for many in the community. Countless numbers paid their rent and avoided eviction because she saved the day, and many more were able to feed their weans after the local bookie took what little money they had. She was, indeed, a legend, although whether she'd have liked the epithet, I don't know. To us, her closest family, she was just Auntie Agnes, extra generous and a fixture at every celebration. When she died at the age of eighty-one, she was sorely missed, or so it seemed.

Sadly, this is where the story takes a darker turn. After Agnes was buried, my family didn't arrange for her to have a headstone, something that shocked me at the time and which has troubled my conscience for thirty-four years. I'll never know why they left her in an unmarked grave. Money wasn't the issue because Agnes's estate, although small by today's standards, was big enough to cover the cost easily. I mentioned it once at the funeral, but the response I got somehow persuaded me to let it go, and I never brought it up again. But I can't forget it.

So, in honour of Agnes, I'm now engaged in tracking down the title deeds for the burial plot, and when I have them, I'll arrange for the erection of a memorial stone. After all these years, some may ask why I'm driven to do this, but the answer is simple: she deserves to be remembered. When strangers pass her grave and see the stone, they'll know she existed, and I believe that's important. After all, she wasn't just my auntie, she was everybody's auntie.

Author note: *My mother died in October 2021, leaving me as the oldest generation in the family. During the time leading up to the funeral, I found many old photographs in her house, many of them taken on holiday in Blackpool, and most of them including Auntie Agnes. I suppose the photos brought a tinge of happiness into what was a sad time, but they also pricked my conscience again because of what happened after Agnes died. That's when I took action and when I put pen to paper.*

Egg and Chips
Sarah Houston

I don't remember how I met them. I don't remember
where. The how and the where are as irrelevant now as
they were then.

The room is crowded and cosy, bright – too bright
– with long plastic strip lights gracing the high white
ceiling. Bob Holness's voice is booming out the big
box of a television which is sandwiched between the
doorway and the fireplace. Each week Bob's contestants
look hopeful and confident. *Blockbusters* is as much a
ritual of this teatime as the egg and chips which I know
will soon be ready.

Evie, short, stout, white-grey, couthie, sits in her easy
chair beside the watery-pictured television set. We
chat comfortably through the game show, about the
questions on the telly and school drama. Bella, a slightly
taller, darker version of her sister, joins the conversation
from the kitchen, just behind the sofa, where she stands,
pinny on, spatula in hand, in front of sizzling pans on
the gleaming white Belling electric cooker.

Bella and Evie: sisters, companions, housemates, my
elderly neighbours from across the road and up the
narrow lane. Every Wednesday after school my little
brother and I head out. Down the gloomy flights of stairs
from our ugly, modern, top-floor maisonette, across the
road, and up the narrow lane to the pretty, old, granite
fishermen's cottages.

Unlike the rest of the cottages, theirs is set side-on
to the lane, with a quaint paved garden to the front,

studded with rose bushes and climbers. A set of well-worn steps leads up from the lane to the garden. It isn't far from where we live, but it's a world apart. The sisters are waiting for us, with a smile and a cup of tea. Six sugars please, says my little brother.

The plates arrive. Bella places them on our knees and sits down beside us with hers. Sometimes we eat at the small dining table in the back corner of the room – just enough space for four. But not today. We eat, watching Bob, trying to answer the questions he asks his contestants, laughing when we get them wrong, mopping up yolk with our chips and sipping sweet, milky tea.

Two elderly sisters. Alone. Together. In the moment of childhood it doesn't even cross my mind to ask if they were married, if they have children, grandchildren, any family to call their own. Each week we follow the egg and chips ritual, without question, without hesitation, without asking. My brother and I know we are welcome.

We moved to this small North East fishing town, our new home, just a few years earlier. It feels like a lifetime ago. My brother and I, and our mum. We knew no one. Our reason for being there is irrelevant now. Our friends and family are hundreds of miles away, somewhere warmer, more familiar. We make some friends but are always incomers.

The language is a challenge: fit like? Loons. Quines. Dookers. It takes a while, but we soon have one way to speak at home, another at school. Playground survival 101.

Many years later. So many things have changed. The place that was strange is now our home. One thing that remains is the warmth in my heart for two lovely ladies, and a plate of egg and chips.

Author note: *The kindness of two elderly sisters towards my brother and me when we were young still warms my heart. I can't think of egg and chips without remembering Bella and Evie.*

In a While, Crocodile
Laura Law

If you had gone to Linlithgow on a particularly cold and windy day in October 2000, you might have come across something resembling a state funeral. The hearse had a police escort and people stopped as the hearse ambled past them. It seemed like half the town crammed itself into the small Catholic church for the funeral mass (despite the majority of the townspeople being either Church of Scotland or not religious at all). Even once all the seats were full, people were standing at the back, craning their necks to see the service. You'd have been forgiven for thinking that this funeral was for a celebrity. It was the funeral of a lollipop lady.

Her name was Teresa, officially, but everyone called her Tess – unless you were a child or teacher at the primary school, then it was Mrs Brown. Still, I know you're wondering how a lollipop lady ends up getting such a brilliant send-off. Maybe you're wondering if it was simply that she was born and bred in Linlithgow? Well, she wasn't. She was from County Tipperary in the Republic of Ireland, and she became part of the 'Forgotten Irish' generation – that is, part of a generation of people where almost half had emigrated to other countries for work and many never went back.

Tess did spend the majority of her life in Linlithgow though. She'd married a local man who she met in London, and they'd relocated to Linlithgow to be near his family. They had five sons together, and in 1972 Tess became a lollipop lady, wielding her big lollipop stick against traffic like Gandalf facing off the Balrog. She carried sweets in her pockets for the schoolchildren (Crème Eggs at Easter), and people have said that she always had a smile on her face or was laughing – except for the time some kids stole her stick, leading her to chase after them, and a week's detention for them. Some people remember being gently scolded as children if they crossed the road where they shouldn't; she'd tell them, 'I'd rather it was me that got hurt than any of you.'

She'd look after kids at the crossing point until she saw their parents turning up, and she crossed at least two generations of children across that one stretch of road. People remember her being there when they were children, and then again when they took their own children to school; some of them ended up working in local shops in Linlithgow as teens and adults, still remembering Tess as always being ready for a blether and a laugh. As for the teachers, one former headmaster recalled how Tess would always greet him with a bear hug and three words that are now etched on the plaque of the memorial bench next to where she stood for work – 'Hello, my honey.'

Tess was my nana, and I was one of the many children she helped across the road on the way to school. I can still picture her now with her yellow hat perched atop her brown perm, her hi-vis jacket down to her knees, and her furry Ugg-like boots – years ahead of the fashion craze that swept the UK in the early 2000s.

I used to visit at weekends, and the pair of us would set off for the shops on the other side of town, her shopping trolley in tow. If it was raining, she had a little plastic cover for her perm, but she always wore the same big, red coat with a golden brooch fastened on her left side, come rain or shine. This journey from her house to the shops was only about twenty minutes on foot, but with her it was an entire daytrip. You couldn't get along the street without bumping into somebody who knew her and who wanted to say hello. By the time we were halfway to the shops, it was usually time for lunch at the Coffee Neuk. Grandad must have wondered what had become of us every week! Sometimes we'd get a bus back if we'd been gone too long, and she always offered the bus drivers a banana or an apple. Everywhere she went in Linlithgow, you would hear, 'Hullo, Tess! How're ye daeing?'

She was sixty-nine when she died – still working, and she was about to go on a trip to London to visit her brothers. The last time I saw her, she was packing for the trip and lent me a book, telling me to give it back to her next time. I had to sit through an entire school assembly where the headteacher talked about my nana and what her loss meant to everyone. After that, the world had a little bit less about it, at least for me.

Over the years since, I've met people who worked with her or knew her in some way, and when I mention her, their faces light up with the memory. I've even had people approaching me just to tell me something about her. The local Facebook page was full of memories from people to mark the twentieth anniversary of her death.

'Tess was genuinely one in a million,' said one man remembering her, and I'm inclined to agree. I've never met anyone quite like her since. She didn't save the world, but she brought love and laughter to it, wrapped up in the cuddly wee package of an old Irish and new Scottish woman.

I've already written about how she used to say hello, but she always used to say for goodbye, 'See you later, alligator.' And you know what? For someone who has never been religious, a part of me hopes I will, so Nana, this one's for you – in a while, crocodile.

Author note: *For* Scotland's Stories, *I thought it was important to tell at least some of the story of Tess Brown, my late grandmother who was an Irish immigrant to the UK, and how beloved she was in her new community, particularly as immigration is part of Scotland's story, and because we are living in a period where immigrants are looked down upon by certain members of society.*

Blue Car

CE Ayr

Ah remember ma mum tellin' us this wan time.

We were a' there, in the livin' room.

Ah can still picture the scene…

*

Ma dad's where he always is, in his chair beside the fireplace.

Ma older brither's still at the table, the bairn's sittin' on the flair beside ma dad, readin' a comic.

He's nine, ma wee brither, but we still ca' him the bairn, 'cause he's six years younger than me, a great wee guy, dead funny, but spoilt rotten.

Ah'm edgin' towards the door, tryin' to escape before ma mum decides she needs help wi' the dishes.

Ah'm already a bit late tae meet ma pal Froggy, an' we're plannin', or raither hopin', tae get up tae a wee bit nonsense the night, mebbe chat up some lassies an' that, it bein' Friday.

Froggy is actually daft enough for anythin', so he is, he's a bit mental, but wi' a heart o' gold, gie you his last penny, so he wid.

He's called Froggy cos he's already ower six fit tall, wi' huge hauns an' feet, but skinny as a rake.

Ma dad says he has the muscle definition o' a plate o' spaghetti.

And he really isnae the smartest, ah huv tae admit.

Limpy Provan, oor English teacher, gie's him a hard time fur bein' thick as mince.

Ah mind this wan time when Froggy had gie'd him a specially dumb reply tae a question, ol' Limpy jist stared at him fur a bit then comes oot wi' this really nasty line.

Does your mother actually feed you, Muir, he asks, or does she just water you twice a week?

Ah had a hard time explainin' that tae him later withoot hurtin' his feelin's.

Tae be totally honest, if his brains were dynamite, he couldnae blaw his nose.

*

Anyway, back in ma story, ma mum speaks.

Mrs Paterson at number 11's man's goat a new car, she says.

Ah should explain somethin'.

Nane o' the men neighbours had names as far as ma mum wis concerned.

And the wimmin a' had a number attached.

No' that it wis necessary, they a' had different names in oor street.

Oh, except for the Wilsons, an' they werenae really in oor wee street, they were on the corners o' the big road.

Ma mum called them Mrs Wilson on the corner, and Mrs Wilson on the other corner.

So their men were called Mrs Wilson on the corner's man, and Mrs Wilson on the other corner's man.

These rules didnae apply to our neighbours.

She wis Flossie next door, and he wis HarryKirby, just the wan word, go figure, eh?

Elaine, who wis five years older than me and a total dreamboat, pure fantasy material, wis Flossie next door's wee lassie, and Johnny, who wis just ma age, wis Flossie next door's boy, that simple.

No' only that, but a' unmarried wimmin were wee lassies tae ma mum, ah don't know why.

Even that Agnes MacKay up the road, number 17, and there's nothin' wee aboot Agnes Mackay, ah can assure yis!

Ah mean, well, yis know whit ah mean, ah'm sure.

*

Okay, back to the story.

Mrs Paterson at number 11's man's goat a new car, ma mum says.

Now ma dad's readin' the paper, of course, like always, and no' really payin' much attention.

He reads it fae the back tae the front, like every man in Scotland, mebbe even the world, ah don't know, because that's where the fitba' is.

Ma mum pauses.

She's great at pausin', ma mum is, she knows jist how long tae pause for.

She watches ma dad, sees him start to notice that she's paused, and he's thinkin' o' what to say, cause he's no' really sure what she wis bletherin' on aboot, then she carries on.

It's blue, she says, dark blue.

Oh aye, says ma dad, which is what he says mebbe 99 percent o' the time.

Dark blue, she says again, what do you make of that?

She's using her posh voice, speaking correctly, to show that we're as good as Mrs Paterson at number 11 and her man even if we haven't got a new car, dark blue or otherwise.

Whit kind is it, ma brither asks, barely lookin' up fae his motorbike magazine.

I have just told you, my mother is getting more posh by the minute, it is dark blue, navy, perhaps.

Naw, says ma brither, whit…

He stops abruptly as ma dad does somethin' that makes the paper snap.

Oh aye, says ma dad, wi' a slightly different inflection this time.

He is nearly as good wi' inflections as ma mum is wi' pauses.

He has aboot fifty-seven variations of 'oh aye' that he uses to suit any situation that might arise.

And a wee movement that might be interpreted as a nod o' the heid, sometimes.

Like now.

Ma mum purses her lips, an' her chin goes doon an' back up.

She is satisfied wi' the family reaction to her news.

She looks at me, gies a wee nod o' her ain towards the dishes.

Ah sigh, but only inside, ah widnae be bad tae ma mum, even if she is gauntae make me late.

Efter a', Froggy'll wait.

Ah nod back.

She pulls the right side o' her cardigan across her chest, then the left side, picks up some plates and marches through to the kitchen.

Ah heap the cups and saucers intae a pile and follow her.

Author note: *I suppose, back in the sixties, we were a normal family, with father working in the factory, at-home mother, kids at school, nobody in jail or on drugs. Not poor, not well-off, just the same as nearly everyone we knew, doing paper rounds and suchlike as soon as we could, and handing the money to my mother. Life was full of moments like this one.*

An t-Òban
Angus Peter Campbell

Nuair a chaidh mo mhàthair
a dh'obair anns na taighean-òsta
bha i am measg nan Gàidheal.
Mòrag,
a bhiodh a' sgùradh nan ùrlair
agus Seonag ag iarnaigeadh gach tubhailt
gus an robh iad a' deàrrsadh geal
mar chlòimh nan uan air madainn earraich.
Eadar aon uair deug is uair feasgar
àm dheth, agus às dèidh na messages a cheannach
fois le cupa tì is siogaireat
ann an 'Refresh' na stèisein
is cabadaich is seanchas is gaol is gàire
ro shioft an fheasgair
agus an uair sin,
gun dùil, aon samhradh,
thàinig Kirk Douglas a dh'fhuireach san taigh-òsta
agus nuair a dh'fhalbh e dh'fhàg e a chuid mhogain
donn is cumanta
a thog i dhachaigh mar dhuais
airson a saothair.

Oban

When my mother
went to work in the hotels
she was amongst Gaels.
Morag,
who scrubbed the floors,
and Seonag ironing all the tablecloths
until they shone white
like the wool on the lambs on a spring morning.
Between 11am and 1 in the afternoon
time off, and after buying the messages
a rest with a cigarette and a cup of tea
in the station refresh
and chat and gossip and laughter and love
before the afternoon shift
and then,
unexpectedly, one summer,
Kirk Douglas came to stay at the hotel
and when he checked out
left his slippers, common grey,
which she took home as a reward
for all her labours.

Machaire Na Hearadh:
A' Fàs is A' Dol Fàs
Mòrag Anna NicNèill

Nuair bhios mi san Àird aig Òrd-Bhàirneach MhicLeòid,
Chan eil sealladh cho àlainn an ceàrn san Roinn Eòrp'.
A' ghrian 's i gam fhàgail 's i deàrrsadh mar òr,
Dol sìos air Àird Mhànais 's air Gàisgeir nan ròn.

Chan eil teagamh nach eil Machaire Na Hearadh na
àite taitneach, agus air iomadh neach a ghluasad
gu bàrdachd, m' athair fhèin nam measg agus an
ceathramh-òrain gu h-àrd a' nochdadh a chuid
fhaireachdainnean gu gleusta, grinn mu mhaise na sgìre.
Tha mi cinnteach gur iomadh duine eile a sheas greiseag
an tacsa na cloiche mòire thar nam bliadhnaichean, agus
a dh'fhidir an smuaintean fhèin mun t-sealladh a bha fo
chomhair an sùilean.

Cuiridh mi geall nam biodh cainnt aig a' chloich, gur
iomadh sgeul a dh'innseadh i fhèin cuideachd. Àrd os
cionn na tràghad air Àird Niseaboist, their cuid gun
robh i uaireigin na h-àite-cruinneachaidh sluaigh aig
Ceann-cinnidh nan Leòdach. Tha seanchas eile ag innse
gun robh i na h-òrd-bhàirneach aig fuamhairean, fada
mus robh sgeul air Clann MhicLeòid. Ach tha fios againn
le cinnt gu bheil i a' dol air ais gu Nua-linn na Cloiche
agus gu bheil i air a bhith a' cumail faire air an àite, air a
socair fhèin, tro na linntean bhon uair sin. Nach iomadh
caochladh a chunnaic i na latha agus air an àrainn mun
cuairt oirre. Daoine a' tighinn is a' falbh, len deòin agus
dhan aindeoin.

Nuair a bha m' athair na bhalach ann an Horgabost, b'
e corra shrainnsear a chìte anns an eilean – gun luaidh
air a' bhaile – agus b' e rud àraid a bh' ann càr fhaicinn
air an rathad-mhòr. Cha bhiodh daoine a' siubhal an uair
sin mar a tha iad an-diugh. Cha robh m' athair ach sia
bliadhna a dh'aois nuair a rinn e fhèin 's a theaghlach an
imrich bho thaobh an ear Na Hearadh gu fearainn ùra
a' Mhachaire, aig deireadh a' Chèitein, 1937. Annas mòr
do ghille beag às Na Bàigh, nach robh air gainmheach
fhaicinn riamh na bheatha gus ceala-deug ron seo,
nuair a thàinig Sgoil Mhànais air chuairt gu Tràigh
Sgarastaigh airson cuirm-chnuic, an latha a chrùnadh
Rìgh Deòrsa VI air an 12na dhen Chèitean.

Rìgh ùr, baile ùr, agus beatha ùr do Dhòmhnall beag
Dòmhnallach. Dòchas às ùr cuideachd, do dhaoine aig
nach robh mòran, agus a rinn riasladh gu leòr a' strì ri
beòshlaint a dhèanamh am measg chreagan is lòin taobh
sear an eilein, far an deach muinntir an taoibh an iar a
chartadh aig àm nam Fuadaichean.

Mean air mhean, dh'fhàs na Machraich ùra cleachdte
ris a' bheatha ùir, agus cha b' fhada gus an robh iad cho
eòlach air a' chruth-thìre choimheach, chòmhnard seo 's
a bha iad air creagan is carraigean nam Bàgh. Ged nach
fhaiceadh iad na steàrnagan a' sgiathalaich os cionn
Sgeir an t-Sruth, bha iad a cheart cho pailt os cionn
Clach MhicLeòid.

Dh'fhàs a' choimhearsnachd cuideachd, is an luchd-
tuineachaidh ùr a' faighinn iasadan de £150 bho
Bhòrd an Àiteachais airson taighean a thogail – agus
80 bliadhna airson a phàigheadh air ais. Ged a shaoilte
an-diugh gur beag-seagh an t-sùim sin, cha robh mo
sheanair a' cosnadh ach beagan a bharrachd air not san t
seachdain aig an àm.

Agus nach iomadh rud a chì an duine a bhios fada beò.

Tha an 80 bliadhna air a dhol seachad, agus ged a tha na taighean an siud fhathast – is tòrr eile a bharrachd air an fheadhainn a thog na croitearan – 's e glè bheag dhiubh a tha nan dachannan.

Ma bha an srainnsear gann nuair a bha m' athair na bhalach beag, chan e sin dheth an diugh anns Na Hearadh. Coltach ri gu leòr de dh'àiteachan eile air a' Ghàidhealtachd is anns na h Eileanan, tha an àireamh dhaoine a tha a' tighinn tro mhìosan an t-samhraidh a' sìor dhol am meud. Tha feadhainn ag iarraidh làithean-saora thall thairis a sheachnadh agus tha feadhainn eile air an tàladh leis na h ìomhaighean brèagha a tha iad a' faicinn air an eadar-lìon. Ge brith dè an t-adhbhar, tha na mìltean de luchd-turais a' taomadh ann a h-uile bliadhna, às gach ceàrnaidh dhen t-saoghal. Ged a tha seo na bhuannachd do chuid, chan eil teagamh nach eil duilgheadas am pailteas na chois do dh'fheadhainn eile. Mar a thachras gu tric is minig, nuair a tha fèill mhòr ga dhèanamh air àite le luchd-turais, tha prìsean nan taighean san sgìre sin a' dol an-àird.

Anns na beagan bhliadhnaichean a dh'fhalbh, chaidh fearainn is taighean is pìosan talmhainn a reic airson prìsean nach fhacas riamh roimhe air taobh siar Na Hearadh. Thathar gan ceannach le daoine nach tig, math dh'fhaodte, ach airson ceala-deug an siud 's an seo tron bhliadhna. Tha taighean eile gan cleachdadh mar dhòigh air airgead a dhèanamh, agus a-nis tha earrann mhath de na taighean eadar Sgarastagh is Losgaintir do luchd-turais a mhàin, no falamh. Cha leigear a leas a ràdh nach eil sin math ann an coimhearsnachd sam bith.

Tha seo gu seachd àraid na dhùbhlan do dhaoine òga, a tha a' sireadh àiteachan-còmhnaidh aig prìsean a tha a rèir an comais – agus tha fios aig a h-uile duine nach seas coimhearsnachd sam bith mura bi daoine òga innte. Tha e doirbh fuasgladh dòigheil fhaighinn air dùbhlan a tha cho ioma-fhillte, ach tha e follaiseach gu bheil turasachd air a buaidh agus a dreach dubhach fhèin a thoirt air an àite.

Aig Sealbh tha fios na tha an dàn dhan Mhachaire san àm ri teachd. Bidh tuineachaidhean gan stèidheachadh is a' dol fàs, agus canaidh cuid gu bheil sin nàdarra gu leòr. Ach tha tòrr a bharrachd an crochadh air coimhearsnachd fhallain, sheasmhach. Tha uallach air daoine gu bheil am Machaire fhèin ga mhilleadh fo chuideam an luchd-campachaidh, ach chan e na dùin-ghainmhich a-mhàin a tha a' crìonadh, agus an cànan is an cultar a-nis ann an staid gu math cugallach cuideachd.

An-diugh, tha talla-coimhearsnachd mòr, ùr na sheasamh os cionn na tràghad, far a bheil an rann a dh'aithris mi aig an toiseach snaighte air leòsain nan uinneag. A-mach orra, chithear Clach MhicLeòid air fàire, shuas air mullach na h-Àirde, fhathast a' cumail faire air a socair fhèin. Cleas nan steàrnag os a cionn, bidh an luchd-turais a' tighinn is a' falbh a h-uile bliadhna, ach tha aon nì cinnteach, am measg gach dùbhlan is iomagain a dh'fhaodadh a bhith againn – 's e sin gum bi a' chlach an siud is gun sgeul air duine againn.

The Harris Machair: Expansion and Desolation

The vista before me at MacLeod's Limpet Stone,
Is the finest in Europe and a joy to behold.
As the sun bids farewell, golden, glistening it shines,
Going down on Àird Mhànais and Gàisgeir, Seal Isle.

The Harris Machair is undoubtedly an alluring place, and one which has inspired many a poet, my own father included. The verse above eloquently encapsulates his feelings as he describes the beauty of the surrounding countryside. I am sure that many others, through the ages, have paused for a moment at the standing stone with their own thoughts and feelings.

I am also sure that if the stone could speak, it would have a fair few tales to tell. High above the beach at Àird Niseaboist, some say that it was once a clan gathering place for the MacLeod chiefs. According to another legend, it was a limpet hammer belonging to the giants of old, long before Clan MacLeod ever existed. What we know for certain is that it dates back to Neolithic times and has been a silent sentinel, quietly watching over the area for centuries. Undoubtedly, it has witnessed innumerable changes through the years as people have come and gone, of their own accord and otherwise.

When my father was a boy in Horgabost, it was unusual to see a stranger on the island – never mind in the village – and it was rarer still to see a car on the road. People didn't travel in those days like they do now. My father was only six years old when he moved with his family from the east side of Harris to the new crofts of the Machair, at the end of May, 1937. A novelty indeed for a little boy from the Bays, who hadn't seen sand until a fortnight before, when Manish School came to Scarista Beach for a picnic, to mark the coronation of King George VI on 12 May.

A new king, a new village and a new life for little Donald MacDonald. Renewed hope as well, for folk who had very little, and who had struggled to make a living amongst the rocks and bogs of the east side of the island, where the people from the west had been driven at the time of the Clearances.

Gradually, the new Machair folk became accustomed to their new lives, and before long were as grounded in this flat, foreign landscape as they had been among the rocks and reefs of the Bays. Although they couldn't see the terns swooping over Sgeir an t-Sruth, the birds were just as plentiful over Clach MhicLeòid.

And, by and by, the community grew and the new settlers were given loans of £150 from the Board of Agriculture to build homes – with eighty years in which to pay the money back. This might seem a paltry sum in today's terms, but my grandfather didn't earn much more than a pound a week back then.

It is said that the man who lives long will see many things in his lifetime. Those eighty years have now passed, and although the houses are still there – with many more, besides the ones the crofters built – very few are homes.

If strangers were thin on the ground when my father was a boy, the same cannot be said of Harris today. Similar to a lot of places in the Highlands and Islands, the number of people now visiting in the summer months has vastly increased. Some want to avoid holidaying abroad, whilst others are attracted by the beautiful pictures they see on the internet. Whatever the reason, thousands of tourists now flock there every year, and they come from all over the world. Although this might be beneficial to some, there is no doubt that it causes problems for others, and when a place becomes popular with tourists, house prices in the area inevitably rise.

Within the last few years, crofts and houses and plots of land have sold for sums never before seen on the west coast of Harris, and are snapped up by people who might only come for a couple of weeks, here and there, throughout the year. Other houses are used as a source of income, and now a significant proportion of the houses between Scarista and Luskentyre are used exclusively by tourists, or lie empty. It goes without saying that this is not good for any community.

The situation is especially challenging for young people who are looking for affordable housing – and everybody knows that a community cannot survive without young people. It is difficult to find a reasonable solution for such a multi-faceted problem, but it is evident that tourism is having an impact, and has cast its own shadow over the place.

Heaven knows what lies in store for the Machair lands of West Harris. Communities settle and disperse, and many would argue that this is just the natural order of things. However, a lot more depends on a healthy and thriving community. People are concerned that the Machair itself is being damaged by the pressure of campers, but like the eroding sand dunes, the language and culture are also in steady decline and in a precarious state.

Today, a large new community hall overlooks the beach, the verse I quoted earlier inscribed on its windows. Looking out, Clach MhicLeòid is visible on the headland beyond, gentle and still, quietly keeping guard. Like the terns above, tourists will come and go with each passing season. We will still have our worries and woes, but one thing remains a certainty – the stone will be there, long after we are all gone.

Making it home

The Seeds of Our Home
Diana Monteiro Toombs

Scotland was not my first home, not even my second.

Like all good love stories, mine was not without its hardships and obstacles to overcome. Moving to Scotland with a small infant in tow and knowing no one at all was always going to be challenging. Despite the beauty and buzz of the city, after many months of living here it still felt unfamiliar. I was, and perhaps still am, a stranger in a strange land.

But slowly it won me over. Gently, over time, it revealed its secrets and offered me a little space in which to plant my flag and start to grow roots of my own.

My Scotland is not a single place. It is a quilt of experiences and memories that have woven themselves into the fabric of my being and added yet another layer to my already eclectic sense of identity.

It is days spent in ancient castles and cathedrals playing with my son, exploring the past and inventing stories and tales of what may have happened there. It is fun and playtime, running through dark passages and spiral staircases and playing knights atop castle walls.

My Scotland is the excitement of sitting in the car and beginning a new adventure to an unknown place. Of embarking on a journey which will ignite the flames of our imaginations, gifting us a feast for our eyes and souls.

It is moments playing on sandy beaches. Squealing, as we talk ourselves into entering the cool waters of the sea and shrieking as we make race tracks in the sand.

My Scotland is laughter as we run across woodlands and embrace the child within. It is pausing to explore the tiny details we might usually overlook and wonder aloud together at what creatures may live there and make the earth their home.

It is collecting shells and stones to treasure as keepsakes of our travels and feature as protagonists in the retellings of our adventures. It is seeds planted with little hope of any chance of growth only to find, a few months later, our windowsills flourishing with colourful flowers and plants that threaten to reach the ceiling.

My Scotland is filled with colour. Beautiful sunsets of purple and pink on short winter days. Red, orange and yellow skies as the sun sets perfectly over a watery horizon. It is bright yellow wellies splashing in muddy puddles and red sledges against white snow. It's filled with yellow gorse on green hillsides and purple heather on autumn days. It is grey stones on a trodden brown path and pink blossom blowing across the window in the spring breeze. My Scotland is aquamarine and deep blue sea against a bone-white sandy beach.

It is landscapes whose grandeur continues to take my breath away. Mountains that rise from the ground like giants, watchers, thousands of years old. Sights that I had only ever seen in pictures, only to discover that the pictures failed to convey their true magnitude and impact.

My Scotland is wild camping and cuddling together as a family in a cramped tent as the wind and rain batter us. It is Glen Coe and forgotten raincoats and campfires. It is ice creams and barbecues besides lochs. It is filled with family walks and attempts to find waterfalls as a small child asks to be carried. It is the renaming of places to Fantasy Hill and Tidy Land.

But more than all that, it is potential and invitation.

Here is the place where we had to begin anew, where we were forced to carve out our own small space and form new habits and traditions. Where we challenged ourselves to confront difficult times and discovered hidden strength and perseverance.

Here is where we took chances. The place where we leapt into the unknown and blindly trusted that we would find a solid landing ground, and we did. The place where dreams were followed and realised, where patience was tested and hypotheticals turned into realities. Here is where we planted new seeds of hope and watched them ever so slowly begin to grow.

My Scotland took time to take shape and form. It did not come easily and was sometimes filled with friction and downright opposition. Sometimes it felt impossible.

But it was patient and let us discover its gifts slowly, in our own time. It welcomed us and with each new experience, rewarded us with an appetite for more. It filled us with a thirst to explore further, to be braver and more ambitious. To make memories that we can treasure long into the future.

My Scotland is not something tangible, but an essence. It is wonderment and hope and inspiration. It is daring to dream. It is the space to pause and appreciate the possibilities before me and finding the courage to seize them when they come. It is trusting in my inner resources and resolve. It is what has turned a foreign land into a home.

Scotland was not my first home. But it is the one which has captured my heart.

Author note: *It had been three years since my husband and I had moved to Scotland with our young son, when we went on a last-minute camping trip to Mallaig. Sitting on the sandy beach in the hot sunshine, I realised that Scotland had truly become my home. The land that had once felt so unfamiliar had now become a part of us, of me, in a way that was as profound as it was intangible. This text is a reflection of those three years, of my relationship to Scotland and of how I came to find and make my home here.*

Pakistani Life in 1960s Glasgow
Lubna Kerr

It was a cold, wet December in 1965. It was only 4pm but it was dark outside as we stepped off the plane. We'd come all the way from Lahore in Pakistan to land in Govan, Glasgow.

My parents left a very comfortable middle-class life in Pakistan when my father was offered the chance of doing a PhD in Chemistry at Strathclyde University.

Our first house was a one-bedroom, fourth-floor tenement flat. My mum, who was pregnant with her third child, had to not only negotiate the stairs but also the comments from our neighbours.

Being a positive person, my mum was able to bat away the questions – 'How come your hair is so dark, do you use coal?' – with her smile, charm and food.

My mum, who was an excellent cook, would fill the tenement close with the aroma of delicious curries. She was an expert in Pakistani cuisine; I wish those genes had been passed on to me. I got the funny genes, my sister got the cooking genes and my brother the software development genes. Luckily we all got the smiling genes.

My father would spend his days researching at Strathclyde University and then work in a factory at night, so that he could help look after his family. He was a very hard-working and clever man. In Glasgow people used the words that we don't hear nowadays. In Pakistan he had taught at one of the best institutions and commanded respect from his students. My father struggled to understand why people would treat him differently just because of the colour of his skin. Racism was a word my parents had never heard or experienced. This caused him a lot of stress.

Like most migrants, my family looked for and found other Pakistani families to share their joys, woes of the weather, food and discrimination.

I remember one Christmas when we went to the carnival at Kelvin Hall. My father tried a baked potato with butter on it for the first time. We looked at him with amazement, fear and some apprehension. He was eating a potato with its skin on, and there were no spices, no colour and no flavour: he took one for the team! We were then treated to candy floss, one between three children (money was tight and teeth were important). Pakistani people have a very sweet tooth, something we have in common with Glaswegians. Have you ever tried a gulab jaman? It's like a deep-fried Mars bar. Gulab jaman is normally served at Pakistani weddings with ice cream; the mixing of cultures, of food and of hope.

Not being able to afford a car but keen to travel and explore our new home, we took bus tours around Scotland. I remember them quite clearly. We children brought down the average age of the tour bus. We went to Stirling Castle, Callander, Inverness and everywhere in between. My favourite trip was the mystery one where you never knew where we would end up. For every trip my mum would make lamb kebabs, unda khakina (a spicy egg omelette) and we would have this with bread and Irn Bru; the mixing of foods and culture were very prominent.

The older occupants of the bus loved having us children around. Well, most did. On the odd occasion we did hear comments about the smell in the bus as my mum would open the tasty food and hand it round the family. It made me very conscious of smells and to this day I am paranoid about it. That is why I always buy the most expensive perfume.

My father loved the Highlands of Scotland. I think it reminded him of his homeland where he had grown up after partition from India, and where he would often visit the Himalayas. Those mountains were slightly higher than our own Ben Nevis. One sunny day, many moons later when we had a car, we climbed to the base camp in our chapals (sandals).

I can still picture the scene: my father walking across the rope bridge, using his hands to hold the wire rope. Then balancing his feet on the single wire that took him across the fast-flowing river below. He reminded me of an acrobat taking his first steps on a high wire; I had never seen a person of colour who was an acrobat. He turned and smiled at us as he crossed. I was so relieved to see him make it back.

My favourite memories of us as a family are of playing cricket in Maxwell Park in Glasgow. My father, the slow-spin bowler, me batting and my siblings the fielders. My poor mum was the umpire, holding on to all our coats with no hands free to sign for a 4 or 6.

Again, a picnic was always part of the joy, eating Pakistani food, samosas, chicken kebabs with chapatis, and, as ever, washing it down with ginger. We'd expanded from Irn Bru to Tizer and Coke.

Because my mum was a great cook, people would never refuse an invitation to eat at our house. My father would invite his colleagues to come to our now two-bedroom tenement flat in Pollokshields for dinner. He was so proud of my mum and how well she had coped with the change in landscape, weather and expectations.

Theirs was a true love marriage, one cut short by the

death of my father at the age of forty-five. He had a massive heart attack caused by stress, discrimination and racism. Strathclyde University named a chemical reaction after my dad when he died, acknowledging the fact that he was a brilliant academic researcher. It is called the Pauson-Khand Reaction. A legacy to be proud of.

My mum lived for thirty-three years after my father died and never looked at another man.

True love can never be underestimated.

Spellbound
Sue Palmer

The house had been on the market for months with no sign of a buyer, so I consulted a witch. She's a friend of a friend and it seemed worth a go.

'Please give me a spell to sell my house,' I asked her. 'The divorce will be through in a week and I'm desperate to move back to Scotland.'

She nodded kindly and told me a spell. So once I got home, I chose a light, airy space – the windowsill in my kitchen – covered it with a golden cloth and placed a leafy plant and a candlestick at each end. Then I hunted around for the final ingredient – something to put in the centre of the magical space to represent my dream of the future.

Unfortunately, most of my stuff was already packed into boxes for the removal people and the best I could do was a jigsaw with a picture on the front of a collie frolicking on a mountainside. I propped the box up against the window and prepared to light the candles, empty my mind of troubles, gaze into the special space and think positive thoughts...

I stood there, trying hard, but it was no good. I couldn't bring myself to get all mystic over a jigsaw box. I didn't even know if it was a Scottish collie.

Time went by. I soon had to leave the country for a couple of weeks' work in the Far East. And, house sale or no, I didn't want to return to Cornwall and all the misery surrounding divorce. So I finished packing and phoned my Cornish friends asking each of them to take me on a favourite walk to say goodbye. It turned out to be a lovely way to bid farewell to them and the county. And on the very last walk, as we scrambled over the crest of a hill, I saw a host of purple thistles, dancing in the breeze...

Back in my kitchen, I strewed thistles around the jigsaw, lit the candles, took a deep breath, emptied my mind of troubles and thought of Edinburgh on a spring morning, with the Castle, Ramsay Garden, the Assembly Hall and all those other glorious buildings banking up into the sky. At which point...

Ding dong! A young couple stood on the doorstep asking if they could see round the house. Within a fortnight we'd completed the sale.

Yes, there really is magic!

Soon the packing cases were all in storage, the car was crammed with everything I'd need to survive until I found a new home, and all the remaining furniture was sold. As I left for the airport, I noticed the thistles still lying on the windowsill. So I took them out to the car and tossed them on the dashboard.

The Far East was exciting, especially since I returned to a hotel room every evening to find email bulletins from my daughter. She'd been reared on stories of Scotland and was utterly besotted with the place, so she'd decided to leave her job and move north with me. She'd already gone up to Edinburgh to stay with a friend and was hunting for a two-bedroomed flat in the city centre. On the day she found one, I was in Hong Kong.

'It's on the third floor but it doesn't feel that high up and it costs a bit more than you said but it's absolutely beautiful, Mum. There are three bedrooms so we can make one into an office. It's really perfect and we must buy it. It's a "fixed price" and bids go in first thing tomorrow. PLEASE, Mum, let me bid!'

Oh well, I thought, why not let your twenty-year-old child spend your every last penny on something you've never seen? I typed 'Yes' and went to bed.

Of course, she managed to be first bidder and, after sorting a money transfer, I left Hong Kong as the owner of a Scottish tenement flat. Over the next couple of weeks, my daughter – bless her – sorted all the legal stuff and bureaucracy, arranged phone, internet and TV, got the packing cases brought up from Cornwall and furnished our new home. When I returned from the Far East I had a few days' work to finish in England but as soon as possible I hurtled up the A1.

Oh, the joy of roaring past the Fàilte Gu Alba sign in the right direction! The Firth of Forth and Bass Rock. Torness power station. Arthur's Seat hoving into view…

In the city centre, I turned off Hanover Street onto cobbles and drew up outside the small blue door I'd seen in the photos. My daughter was already installed up there – all I had to do was press the buzzer.

With a muttered thank you to the witch, I opened the car door – then noticed the dried-up thistles lying on the dashboard.

'Oh God,' I said. 'This is Thistle Street!'

Yes, there is magic. Every word is true. And as I write this story I'm celebrating my fifteenth year in this lovely place.

On a Sense of (s)p(l)ace
Raman Mundair

When we are born our sense of self is tied to the bodies that surround us. The folks we consider parents or parental figures. We feel a visceral connection to them, they feel so strongly a part of us that we cannot imagine our place in the world without them. As we grow, we form other attachments. Little strings of connection between us and people, music, moments. Little strings that form webs. Webs that structure and hold suspended our senses of self. Later we anchor ourselves to lovers, friends and experiences. As we get older, a sense of emotional geography emerges. A personal cartography of all the actual physical places that embody our experience. The house we were raised in. The tree we climbed. The tree we fell out of. The house where we realised we no longer belonged.

The default orientation to this is that these experiences and moments happen to us, at us, that we have no autonomy over the creation of our own emotional geography. That the sense of home and place in our personal cartographies are born out of a fateful reckoning. But what if we could be proactive and fashion our own sense of home and place? If we could carry this inside us, our own personal estate that we protect and nurture and that couldn't be taken from us?

When I was a child I used to dream of secret gardens. Night after night I would imagine that I had lucked upon an opening in my parents' prosaic garden, a wormhole that I stepped through, 'Alice'-like, into another world. A world similar to mine but much better.

My secret garden was less about a potential physical space but more about a space opening up inside of me. A place where I felt more myself, away from the tyrannies of childhood and the daunting prospect of young adulthood, where I was safe and free to dream. In this garden I was a concentrated self, a pure essence of my spirit – in the garden I was 'me'.

I've lived in Shetland for many years and experienced the wild landscape as if it were a dear, challenging friend that facilitated growth. In fact I felt married to the landscape and more connected to it in a way that I didn't with the island people. I found many private spaces and places that felt like home, including a friend's semi-cultivated garden – Lea Gardens. This special place has at times felt to me a secret escape – an unbelievable lush imagining in a landscape which can sometimes feel unwelcoming. Lea Gardens is a horticultural triumph and a delight to the eye in every season. It's a place where one can be more of one's self – concentrated and mindful in the here and how. What is a garden if not a place of endless possibility? What is a garden if not a sanctuary, a place that restores, renews and reveals new ways of being?

Lea Gardens is an extraordinary place. A poetic testimony of how one can create one's own environment in horticultural grammar and metaphor. A creative intervention in the Shetland landscape that sings and speaks to us of how we can embed ourselves peacefully, respectfully and playfully into the landscape. How we can endeavour to dialogue with nature in a way where we draw out the accent rather than clip its joyful cadence and its contribution to the natural, open song of the North.

Here the garden's textures, layers, stillness and activity all offer space to ponder beauty, the seasons, the cycles of life and a place for self-restoration. A sacred space to suit yourself, reflect and to look inwards and feel home rather than looking outwards, looking and yearning for home. You are home, you are here and in this moment the Shetland curlew's song is mine. The heather, moss and undulating hills and skies are mine.

I am not particularly religious, but I do feel a spirit connection with nature. To the curlew and the bonxie. The sparrow and the wren. The sea and sky are reflections of my ever-changing mind and mood. Trees offer sacred sanctuary. Flora and fauna delight the heart and eye. All feed and uplift my spirit. I am a nature girl. Despite the fact that I lived in cities for most of my childhood, I am truly at home when in natural and rural spaces.

I was born in India, but raised in the UK. When I returned to India for the first time in my early twenties, I was struck by how viscerally I connected with rural India. India is so diverse – there are many, many aspects to India, each so different. For me, returning to the place where I was born, Punjab, and visiting the land of my ancestors, the pind, rural Punjab, was a revelation. Everything made sense. How I felt so at home with nature, in all its forms.

I understood that the heart of me was a country girl. That although I loved the city and city life, on many levels cities were like mistresses who drew me away from my true love, my true self, my real life. I have felt nurtured by both cities and the country but in one space, I felt I had head and heart space and in the other, I often felt unable to discern my own wants and thoughts from others. Cities were inspiring, entertaining and exciting but were for me a place of bamboozlement. They provided a diversion from myself.

Interestingly, what I miss most about cities are people and the best of what humanity can make: art, music, food and community. I don't have that human connection in remote, rural island life, but what I do have is head and heart space and a pure conduit to nature. In the natural world, in wildness, I feel my true size and imagine I have a more accurate perspective on life. Recent years spent split between Shetland and Glasgow's Southside have proved fruitful. Last year I was proud to be part of the community that actively stopped a UK Immigration and Borders Protection agency taking one of our neighbours. That May day on Kenmure Street will never leave me and has been banked as one the (s)p(l)aces in my heart that will never be displaced. I feel emotionally tethered to the truly gallus and green locale of Pollokshields in a way that I never thought any city could seduce me. Scotland's Shields and Shetland Islands have shaped, nurtured and uplifted my current neuro-pathways in these days of flux, and I am forever grateful for this.

Walls
Margaret Grant, Paisley Creative Writing Group

When I came back that day
after everything had happened, I thought
you didn't remember me.
We were your first guests after all
and you took care of us.
I could see you shivering
in the January chill as I ran from the car
the weeping snow
slipped the key in the lock.
Inside you were pink-blue cold.
We said our hellos
your hand in mine
formal and firm, still
an ocean of memory
between us.
I wandered
I wandered your days your years
sank into the echoes of
dreams coloured
rainbow bright
drank laughter
spilling like spring showers.
I caught the whispers of time
opening their wings
learning to fly hinged
to this family of mine.
I heard the doors to our heart flutter
as night came.

Too soon
a man has come
to take measurements, photographs
make notes.
How could he know
the pockets of these walls brim
full with treasure.
Tell him, walls,
tell him.
Others will come.

Author note: *Does our childhood home keep our
memories? I think it does. In January 2000, I sat in the
living room of my parents' house waiting for the estate
agent. My mother had died the previous November,
while the world was gearing up to celebrate the new
millennium. As I flicked through a newspaper listening
for a knock at the door, the house stirred my memories
and I found myself upstairs – a movie of my childhood
with my two older sisters playing before my eyes.*

Origin stories

Because Ah Matter
Angel Rodgers

Like a rat up a drainpipe, I shot oot that school gate lik'
the devil was on mah tail. This wasnae mah gig, an' Ah
wasnae unpacking. If Ah was gonnae engage in education
anywhere, it wasnae here. Ah totally had the fear, an'
the battle lines between me and mah maw were drawn.
Day in, day oot, Ah was frogmarched through the gate.
Opposing the forces at play, Ah shot right back oot it.

'Get back here!' Gangly Gibson with the protruding
teeth stomped a path towards me.

'It's no happenin!'

'We'll see!'

'Come at me, tin-opener teeth, ya absolute howler!'

Gibson snatched mah arm. In the tussle she
somersaulted backside over elbow an' splattered
spreadeagled on the concourse lik' an upturned turtle.

Thirteen years an' a prolific school-refuser, Ah wis
a gob on legs wi' a tongue that held enough spark tae
light a match. Filterless, mah thoughts tripped oot mah
mouth. Focused and fearless, Ah thought they were
justified. If there wis ever a Holy Grail ae rebellion, then
Ah wrote the book. Defiance, not compliance, that was
mah motto. There wis nae taming this free spirit. Why?
Because Ah matter.

'School..., or Ah'll get the jail!' mah maw wis at her
wits' end.

'Orite Greta Garbo..., curb yir melodramatics!'

At war wi' society, Ah rolled wi' mah posse, much tae
her disapproval. Ah wasnae caring, they were mah pals.

Ah was accepted an' ready tae roll wi' whatever.

Pals or nae pals, Ah wis a one wuman yippin', chippin' nightmare. Regarded the family disappointment, Ah acknowledged Ah wis an organic pain in society's rectum, but debated Ah wis a product ae the soil she'd fertilised me in.

The day the polis chapped, her mania skyrocketed.

'Get yir carcass tae school!' PC Bobbin roared on his unannounced visit. 'Yer maw's demented wi' ye!'

Blanking him, Ah gaped oot the windae an' scanned the expanse ae Jubilee Crescent.

'Whit's she doin'?' he squinted.

'Lookin' for who asked you!'

'Shift yirsel' lady!'

'Eh, that'll be a naw ya absolute fraggle!'

Faking bravado, I darted away an' locked myself in the lavvy as Bobbin pounded the hallway in hot pursuit.

'Ya cheeky wee...!'

'Gon yirsel' ya mutant!' I called fae mah hideout. 'Remove your boggin' breath fae mah maw's keyhole wi' immediacy, it reeks like a hog's butt!'

Shots fired, the stench ae fear rose as Bobbin and mah maw battered the door dementedly.

'Sorry officer!' mah maw squirmed. 'Ah'm affronted wi' her!'

'And thar she blows in three-two-one..., gon' yirsel' Maw!'

'Your jaiket's on a shoogly peg!' she went from a steady simmer to near-explosion in point four ae a millisecond, hammerin' the door lik' a wuman possessed.

'Hawd yirsel' together!' I cranked it up a gear, the door bolt ensuring mah safety. 'Yir embarrassin' yirsel' in front ae the constabulary!'

A stilled silence ensued as the stand-off continued.

'She's disturbed!' mah maw sighed.

'Aye… pot, kettle hen!'

'Well, yir brother's no lik' that!'

'Aye, Ah'm totally killin' the whole family disappointment thing!'

The rebellion held out as Bobbin admitted defeat when his radio crackled, an' his gaffer ordered him elsewhere. Nane-the-less, rebel was trending, an' like an infection, Ah took hold.

Exiting mah hideout, Ah prepared for the onslaught. In an ugly incident, if looks could have killed, Ah was a goner. No' the height ae nonsense but famed for her signature daggers, mah maw drew her eyes aff me, the look penetrating my soul.

'Yir grounded!'

'An' that'll no' be happenin'!' I winked.

'Gerrin!'

'Naw…, tally-ho, Maw!'

'You're a pure riot!' ma posse chuckled as Ah relayed rebel events.

Ah was a complex kid but so was mah fear. Life had torn cracks in mah maw cos ae her poor choices and she wasnae getting away wi' tearing any more cracks in mine. A victim ae circumstance, mah rebellion rose fae frustration from our midnight flit tae Edinburgh, and being catapulted without warning intae a life Ah didnae fit intae. Mah broad Glaswegian accent made me the subject ae ridicule. So did the clothing grant shoes and jacket, indicating Ah was a welfare wean, that made me the subject ae playground humiliation. They were bouffin', they compromised mah dignity, an' Ah wasnae wearing them.

Wi' the dreaded chap fae Peacock, the Education

Welfare Officer, trouble brewed. An imposing character, he terrorised weans. No' this wean though. The stand-off continued until he put me before the Children's Hearing.

Sat in silence, the glare ae the opposition wis slicing.

'Awkward!' I blurted out amid disbelieving gasps.

'Show some respect!' the bigwig peered over his spectacles.

'Bolt you, ya fossil!'

Fit to explode, mah maw feigned patience. She had tae, there were too many witnesses.

'You poor woman!' the bigwig sniffed.

'Hawd on..., how's she the victim? Ye havnae asked mah side ae the story!'

'Just go to school!'

'Aye... so an' Ah will!'

Losing the battle, a Compulsory Supervision Order was imposed and Ah was appointed a fangly dangly Social Worker. Let me tell ye, that wis never gonnae work. Somethin' in mah soul cried an' Ah rose in resistance.

'Ram yir Social Worker, ya bampot!'

Ah didnae fit intae the new world, an' they wernae gonnae make me.

Life never gave me lemons, it turned me upside down an' smacked mah backside, leavin' scars naebody noticed. Social Worker or no, Ah never returned tae school. It's changed days though. Although the hardliner rebel still bubbles within, Ah turned failure intae success, an' made peace wi' mah demons. A practising Social Worker, Ah support weans lik' Ah wis. The difference: these weans have a voice.

Lookin' back, mah maw had her misgivings, but so did Ah. Throughout the battles, her patience wis commendable. What she didnae see wis that Ah had inherited her fighting spirit.

All misrepresented rebels, salute yirselfs, live fast, rebel hard, regret nowt an' stand up for what ye believe in, even if yir standin' alone. Why? Because ye matter!

Author note: *As a teenager living in the west of Scotland, my family fled significant domestic violence in the early 1980s. To get on the school bus one morning to be told without warning, or a chance for an ending or the opportunity to say goodbye was detrimental to my outcomes. Plummeted into a life I did not fit into, I battled the systems at play. Children didn't have a voice back then and with social justice burning in my soul I became a Social Worker to ensure kids could be heard.*

Epona
Elizabeth Craig

I remember going over
a bridge with my father.
The Clyde's muddy waters
flowed swirling below.
The everyday world
was left far behind us
and lying before us
the new and unknown.
I remember a smiddy
a huge humid cavern
a hammer's loud clang
metallic and sharp.
A fire spitting sparks
to the breath of the bellows
the flicker of flames
in the unquiet dark.
I remember a horse
that shone in the darkness
its coppery coat
reflecting the flames
its mane a corona
of light and of fire
backlit by the furnace
and flowing untamed.
I remember the scorching
the smell and the smoke
the wild rolling eyes
as the horse tossed its head

the hot steaming shoes
hammered home by the smithy
my dad's hug dispelling
my feelings of dread.
I was only a child then
not knowing such words as
astonished amazed
or spiritualised.
And nor did I know
that this numinous scene
would shine in my mind
for the rest of my life.

Epona – Celtic/Roman horse goddess

Author note: *I have never forgotten this scene. Crossing
the Clyde on the bridge was a great adventure as I was
very small. I was completely awed by the scene in the
blacksmith's workshop, viewed through the wide open
doors. It was the first time I recognised the sentient
aspect of an animal's existence, and my first spiritual
experience.*

Dear

ED Robertson

If I stare at this sheet of white paper for much longer I'll
have snow blindness. I pick my pen up again. I want to
do this, I do, but I don't know what to say or even how
to begin. Dear... who? This letter is my chance to make
a good first impression so I want to get it right. Well, my
first impression as an adult. We've met before, but a long
time ago. I have no idea what kind of impression I made
then. I sigh. I know that if I don't get started soon, I'll
lose my nerve and this won't get done at all. Will I regret
that, I wonder.

I think about the journey to Edinburgh, feeling
nauseous and overheated, my baby moving and kicking
in my belly, in time to the movement of the bus, nudging
me, with wee waving elbows and wee kicking feet, as he
or she had nudged me to begin this journey. The idea of
finding out about my adoption, about my birth family,
grew as my baby and my belly grew. It was strange, the
way this need for information, for contact, had come
over me, a real pregnancy craving, stronger than the
need for choc chip ice cream at 8am.

I was glad to get out of the bus and to feel the cold,
fresh blast of December air. But I soon realised what
a stupid idea it had been to come into the heart of
Edinburgh on the Friday before Christmas. Crowds of
Christmas shoppers marched along Princes Street and I
braced myself to walk against the shopping tide. I pulled
my heavy red woollen coat around me in the hope that it
would protect my bump from flying shopping bags and
sharp shoppers' elbows.

I found the building I was looking for, hiding in plain sight at one end (or maybe the beginning) of Princes Street. New Register House, home of records and secrets, including my own. I walked in, in awe of the building and its contents, in awe of the tumult of mixed feelings I was experiencing. I waited, impatiently, uncomfortably, while my document was located. Eventually I was invited into a small grey room. It felt wrong to be receiving such big, bold new information in such a small, bland space. Then I was informed that I could not have it. I was shocked. Surely I was entitled to see my own original birth certificate? I had presented my adoption certificate and proof of my identity. But my identification was in my married name. Although I had been married for seven months, and was now used to having my husband's name and being this new married, pregnant person, I hadn't anticipated that my marriage certificate wouldn't have caught up with me. I'd arrived here before my paper documents had. So they could not accurately verify my identity. So no birth certificate, no knowledge, for me. I couldn't bear the unfairness of this, of the clerk having my details right there yet not handing them over. I felt faint. The clerk, probably about my own age, wavered. He made his decision just before I had to cry. He must have wanted rid of this heavily pregnant, heavily emotional woman. He handed over the piece of paper, explaining why he shouldn't be doing this and justifying why he was. But I was not listening. I was reading greedily, giddily. I read my mother's name. I read my father's name: unknown. I saw my first, my original name. In all the time I had thought about what my name could have been, this one had never entered my head. I felt disappointed in myself that I had no intuition about this. This new/old name made me feel strange, alien, disoriented, like I was, or could have been, a different person entirely. A person called Caitlin.

My baby nudges me again. So I take a deep breath and begin.

Hi,

I hope you are well and that this letter does not come as too much of a shock. I am Caitlin. [Should I write 'your daughter'? No, too demanding. But what if she knows another Caitlin. I'll tell her my age and hopefully she'll put two and two together and work it out.] *I am 21 now, married and pregnant. It's really being pregnant that's made me think about looking for you and contacting you, apparently this is very common. It started at antenatal appointments, when they ask about family medical history and I had to say I didn't know any, and it grew from there.*

I've had a very happy life with my mum and dad. I've always known I was adopted and I was content with that knowledge and with the life I have. And I didn't want to risk upsetting you or your life now. I know that things were very difficult for single mothers when you had me and I realise that it could not have been easy for you.

I'll not write any more just now as I expect I've given you enough to think about. I hope you decide to contact me but I will understand if you decide not to.

[How do I finish the letter now? I can't write 'love' and I can't write 'yours sincerely'.]

Thank you for reading this.

Ella

[X or no x? X might be too much, too soon, too much expectation. But no x might seem cold, clinical, matter of fact. I don't know.]

X

Inspired by Ladybirds
Linda Brown

A neighbour handed two second-hand books into my gran's house.

'They'll keep the wean entertained when she comes tae visit, Mary.'

Gran, an established member of the hand-me-down generation, accepted them with thanks, adding them to my reading pile on her bookshelf.

The books, both published around 1961 – *The Ladybird Book of Trees* and *What to Look for in Spring* (a Ladybird Nature Book) – fascinated me from the moment I flicked through their well-thumbed pages. I was hooked by the bright illustrations and engaging text. I yearned to be able to identify trees. Know when to listen for willow-warblers and where to look for blackthorn blossom.

Even at eight years old I realised the books' content and tone were aimed at a Famous Five kind of child. A 1950s girl from 'doon south', who enjoyed spiffing adventures, drank lashings of ginger beer and ate something mysterious called radishes with her salad. Not a wee 1970s lassie fae an Ayrshire lace toon, who kicked about the swing park, drank red kola and ate chips with her salad. Some of the idyllic landscapes portrayed on the pages – marshlands, downs and canal-banks – would not be discovered on my doorstep. Lombardy poplars were hardly flourishing in my local woods. Reed warblers and sandpipers were unlikely to be nesting along the nearby river... or were they?

Undeterred by these minor concerns, I took the books home, rounded up four pals and organised an expedition for Saturday. The plan was to explore our Irvine Valley 'backyard' searching for the trees, plants and wildlife described and illustrated inside the Ladybird books.

So, on a fine spring morning, our own little Famous Five gang – Lynn, Cathy, Ann, Beth and I – set out with my books shoved in a duffle bag, along with a handful of Highland penny caramels for sustenance.

Our first foray into the wilds took us to the woods on the bank of the River Irvine, just a stone's skim from the village centre. Eyes alert for signs of wildlife, we meandered through the trees, studying bark and leaves, comparing them with the drawings in the books. Someone had brought a small magnifying glass to help. Soon, we were identifying beech and sycamore trees, spotting blue tits and chaffinches flitting among the branches, inhaling the oniony scent of wild garlic and spying grey wagtails bobbing about stones at the river's edge.

We followed the path to Newmilns Dam. On previous walks there with my parents, when the river had been in spate, I'd caught glimpses of sleek silver skin and thrashing tails in the frothy waters, as salmon struggled to loup the dam, battling to reach their spawning grounds upstream.

But that day, the river was low and calm. All we saw in the shallows beyond the dam were darting shadows of brown trout.

Over that spring and summer we five explorers rambled around the countryside surrounding our town. We hunted for wildflowers, finding red campion and marsh-marigolds clustered on boggy ground, where, to great hilarity, Beth lost a shoe and gained a muddy sock. We were stung by nettles. Searched for soothing docken leaves. Shins and calves stained green, we stripped off socks and shoes and paddled in the chilly crystal waters of a burn. Pebbles jaggy beneath our toes, tiny fish tickling our ankles. We roamed Big Wood, renowned in late spring as a bluebell paradise – and nicknamed locally as Bluebell Planting. Thousands of the iconic flowers were spread like a violet cloak across the woodland floor. An abundance of bluebells can indicate ancient woodland, dating back centuries, and certainly Bluebell Planting has a strong connection to Ayrshire's past. Deep among the trees, alongside a burn and being reclaimed by nature, are the ruined remains of the twelfth-century motte and bailey of Arclowden Castle – reputedly the home of Lady Margaret Crawford, mother of William Wallace.

Folklore suggests that bluebell woods are enchanted; bluebells are said to ring to summon fairies. But we never heard any bells or saw any fairies. We only heard beautiful birdsong and saw squirrels scampering up oak trees to hide in foliage and the white scuts of rabbits disappearing among the flowers.

Fifty years on, and I still walk these riverbank and woodland paths. Not much has changed. Some trees have gone and the dam has long since been demolished, but the bluebells blossom at Big Wood – still a magnificent blue-purple haze stretching as far as the eye can see.

Nowadays I take my camera with me on my rambles, snapping shots of snowdrops and thistles, herons and hares, flowering hawthorn and ripe brambles. Only last week, I was overjoyed to capture my first image of a kingfisher, vivid amber and teal, regally perched on a low branch overhanging the Irvine, a fish clamped in his beak.

Without doubt, those old Ladybird books sparked my curiosity, inspiring a lifelong love of nature and I've happy memories of our innocent childhood treks of the 1970s, when we experienced a taste of freedom and independence our own children a few decades later would not be allowed.

And what happened to my Ladybirds? Well, I still have them. And treasure them. My own kids enjoyed them too.

Today, their dustcovers are long missing and their yellowed pages exude a slight musty odour. But they are tucked away, top shelf, on my hall bookcase.

Patiently waiting to be handed down to my future grandchildren.

Author note: *My love of my local environment and its wonderful nature stems from my childhood rambles, and was inspired by two hand-me-down Ladybird books which I still treasure today.*

The Berries
Angela Logan

'Dinnae leave the soap in the basin, lassie, you'll waste it!'

I sing-song an obedient, 'Okay, Granny!' rescuing the slimy bar of soap from the plastic bowl of creamy water and placing it to one side, on the dry grass.

I reach for the sweet-smelling, sun-bleached towel and scrub my still slightly soapy face pink, using the rough texture to clean the worst of the dark red stains from my damp fingers before running off to join cousins and cousins of cousins out in the field.

Nearly every summer holiday, between the ages of three and fifteen, I would trade ballet classes, Sunday School and life as I knew it, for The Berries.

The Berries was an alternate reality where streetlights, video games and TV were replaced by gas mantles, playing cards and campfires. It was a world away from the life of a wean in Central Fife, who was good at the school and always had her nose in a book. It was a wilder, less predictable place and time, where anything could and, more often than not, did happen.

My mother's family are Scottish Gypsy Travellers – that's an officially recognised ethnic minority now, one to tick on forms and wear proudly as part of your heritage – it always was to us anyway.

There was never a build-up to this alternate universe. One day, after school, we'd all bundle into the backs of cars, pick-ups and the ubiquitous Transit vans, towing a range of trailers. Always trailers, never caravans –

caravans were what Scaldies used for holidays – The Berries was not a holiday.

'Mind now, you need tae work hard and no shame me. I was always the best picker when I was wee, well, except for your Auntie Betty,' my mother reminds me, with an air of dignity and deference to her oldest sister.

'Aye, Mammy, I'll pick hard,' I reply.

Mum always became 'Mammy' at berry time, I didnae want to stand out like the wee half-breed buck I was. I was used to it, my father's distinctly non-Traveller family were from Belfast where I was a half-breed of a different kind; one who never talked about childish fantasies of becoming a nun and obediently waiting until the National Anthem was finished before turning the TV off at night. Fitting in was a well-practised art; one I took satisfaction in.

The small convoy of motors and wee trailers would head north, in the general direction of Perth, after stopping for a full tank of diesel at a cheaper Fife garage. We'd pull in at a camp, usually a big field owned by the farmer whose berries we'd come to pick – it had to be a big field because there would be hundreds of us pulling in over the next while – and the season would begin.

The ritual of picking berries is a rare privilege that I still miss. Up early, pull on your picking clothes in the fresh morning air, clothes that would become purple from the juices on my hands and in my buckets as the summer progressed. Someone would have made a piece – usually meat paste or cheese on plain bread with a packet of crisps each and a pack of biscuits to split at piece time. My mammy and aunties would bring a flask of tea and the weans would have a big bottle of diluted juice, made with the water we'd fetched from the tap that morning. Some of the best meals I ever ate were eaten from an old margarine tub, sitting on a luggie, at the top of my dreel.

We'd pick all day, mostly in the heat of the sun, with bees humming around us and the scent of camomile and summertime heavy in the air. I usually had a cousin as a picking partner. We'd pass time singing songs or retelling stories that we'd overheard the big ones tell the night before.

We'd get distracted and, despite the fact our mothers couldn't see over the top of the dreel either, we'd occasionally hear a soft but ominous, 'Get pickin' lassies!' come from nowhere... how did they know? They'd tell us they had eyes in the back of their heads but the wisdom of motherhood tells me it's probably because they'd done the very same thing, a generation ago.

For a small child, night-time on the camp was magical. The expanse and variety of the beautiful Perthshire countryside was our kingdom, we'd have adventures immersed in the sights, smells and other sensations that children access with such ease.

If we could stay up until dark, we'd become privy to all the secrets and scandals of adult life. It's remarkably easy for a quiet wean to go unnoticed, just out of the light of the campfire. I'd listen to stories told by tired aunties and uncles who were grateful for the warmth of both the fire and the connection with much-missed friends and family, after a hard day's work. When sleep arrived, it usually happened head-to-toe with a cousin or younger auntie in a single bunk, with the sounds of the men, still round the campfire, softly chattering away.

The summer would continue in this endless way, punctuated, on Saturdays, by a trip to 'The Toon' for which we'd be scrubbed and dressed in our good clothes. The Toon was Blairgowrie and, boy or girl, we'd be splashing about in the Ericht in our underpants by afternoon, with a promise of chips and ice cream for supper if we were good.

Somehow, late August would arrive and we'd pack up to make the journey back to Fife. The old empty sock I brought to safely stash my berry money in would be full to bursting with my earnings, just waiting to be spent on fancy back-to-school stationery that I would proudly use in the static boxes that muffled my voice and the static routines that muffled my freedom. Until next year.

Author note: *As a child, I was always a bit of everything and not quite enough of anything specific. This fundamentally shaped my experience of life and made me more open to difference in the world – I have since learned that this 'not quite belonging' is a defining part of many of the stories of Scotland.*

Something Precious?
Vivien Jones

'Town centre – Christmas – purse in your handbag? No chance.'

The policewoman couldn't have been less interested. She wrote down my details, gave me her email, saw me out of the police station as quickly as she could. The bank clerk was more sympathetic as I cancelled my cards.

'Anything precious besides your cash and cards?'

Oh yes.

*

The thing was, I hadn't wanted another doll episode. Grandma's sly favouritism towards my older sister still rankled. It's true she kept her socks clean for longer and she didn't lose her hair ribbons, but it still wasn't fair. Two dolls, one more beautifully clothed, more curly-haired than the other. One dressed in white silk, the other in yellow cotton. One with white leather boots with tiny studs, the other in knitted bootees. One in glitter wrapping, the other in Father Christmas paper. If we had the same thing it was bound to happen again. So I thought of something different. Grandma had already asked for our Christmas lists.

I thought Daddy would be a better bet than Mummy. I started to talk at teatimes about trains. I drew lots of trains in my drawing book. I asked if we could go and watch the trains pass by from the hill above the line. Finally, I mentioned I would quite like a train set for

Christmas.

My sister spluttered her tea and Mummy scolded her. My little brother said, 'Can I play, Vivi?' But he said that all the time.

'Thought you wanted a cradle for your dolls, you two,' Mummy said.

'Well, I'm certainly not having a train set,' added my sister. 'That's a boy's toy.' She laughed and they all joined in.

Grandma must have laughed too, for on Christmas morning under the tree lay two boxes, one in gold paper, the other in silver. My sister's cradle had flowers stencilled on the headboard, mine had shapes. Hers was white, mine was yellow. Grandma was there, of course, though I only remembered three Christmases so far, she was always there to enjoy her giving. We did thank you and powdered cheek kisses, then turned for our main presents from Mummy and Daddy. Daddy had gone to the other room but my sister couldn't wait. She opened a huge box and lifted out a push-chair just the right size for her doll. There was a quilt and a pillow with a frill and even a sunshade. She glowed. My brother ripped open his box and cooed with delight. It was a carpenter's set with bright coloured blocks, all different shapes, and a tin of tacks and a wooden hammer. Mummy showed him that the blocks were already pierced and he began hammering straight away. 'Making something,' he said proudly.

I couldn't see my box. I looked at Mummy and she looked a bit anxious, like when she's made something new for supper and she doesn't know if we're going to like it. Daddy came through and crooked a finger at me. 'This way, little lady,' he said. So I followed him into the dining room. I gasped.

On the carpet lay a single circle of track. On the track sat a green engine, a black coal truck and a brown goods wagon. I leaned closer and saw they were joined up by little hook and eye links. Daddy took one hand from behind him and handed me a metal key. It looked like an elephant's head with huge eyes. He pointed to the hole in the side of the engine. 'Try it,' he said. So I put the key with its square hollow onto the square shaft in the engine and felt it tense as I turned it. I set it back on the track. I thought I heard it hum with excitement but perhaps it was me. Daddy pointed to a lever in the cabin. I flicked it. And the train went. Round and round and round and Daddy laughed and I laughed and the others came in and laughed too, Grandma and my sister because they thought it was a silly present, my mother from relief, my brother because everyone else was laughing, and me and Daddy for joy. He bent his knees and took his other hand from behind him. In it were a pair of V-shaped pieces of track. 'They're points,' he said. And my daddy and I put our smiling heads together and bent over my Triang Hornby train set and took out the metal brackets and fitted the V-shaped pieces so my train could go round the track or across an S-shaped route in the middle. And it never crashed once. And that was my best Christmas Day ever.

*

Oh yes.

In my black leather purse along with the mere cash and cards had been my Triang Hornby key, the symbol of my first independence, my first passion, my irreplaceable treasure. The trinket that had been explained to friends and lovers through the years, received with smiles, a little mockery sometimes, was gone. Tossed into a bin with the purse, the Japanese God of Luck token, and all the other things of no importance.

Something inside me lost my last grip on childhood and this sixty-five-year-old wept in the street.

Author note: *I was Christmas shopping in a thronging Dumfries town centre – went to pay for something and had that awful shock you get when you can't find your purse. Searched over and over but knew right from the start it was gone.*

The Jakit, Mysticism n PPK Resurrection

Graeme Armstrong

The Boys' Brigade wis on a Friday night up oor bit. Ma maw said that they put it on then tae keep boys aff the streets cos the weekends wur mad here. We wur in Anchor Boys in the church hall n somebody opened the door n flung a firework in. It flew across the floor n exploded against the back wall. A thought it wis quite excitin but the boys standin nearest it wur greetin n the leader wuman said they got some fright. The polis came n aw that, so they did. There wis a big UVF 1690 spray-painted on the wall ootside n there wis always broken glass in the lane. Yi used tae pass a gang ae troops standin at the toll wae green bottles wae yella labels n wae lassies aw laughin n carryin on. We used tae go tae Sunday School in the same hall tae learn aboot the bible n aw that. A remember askin a teacher tae explain Christ's atonement in mare detail, like expand it oot kinda thing. *How did Jesus die for oor sins? Like, why but?* N they said, cos he just did n A left confused n unsatisfied. It is complicated stuff tae explain, right enough. It wis in Sunday School we received the first subtle messagin aboot social stratification. Heaven doesnae discriminate. Angels appear tae shepherds n Magi n maybe even tae boys or girls wae an extra stripe on their trainers. We dressed up as donkeys n wise men in the nativity but still remained oblivious tae redemption n salvation. A broke ma VL in the hall at a disco absolutely smothered in Lynx Voodoo wae a

DJ playin aw the eld bangers like PPK 'Resurrection' n aw the wee burds came heavy dolled up. Panda pops, Frosties n Spicy Bikers tuck shop material. Some howl.

First thing in the Company Section fur elder boys wis a trip tae the Isle ae Arran. We hud the school camp just before it. A marched aboot Dounans in a pair ae black Cat boots n a pair ae DPM poly-cotton army troosers wae the school. Ma feet wur rid raw... so fur this wan, ma maw said A needed proper walkin boots n took me tae Tiso in Stirling tae hire a pair. The madness ae the streets hud awready started. A hud ma eye on a Berghaus Mera Peak jakit, no fur hill walkin but fur kickin aboot wae the young team. A chanced ma arm n said, *Mum, this Goatfell is a meaty peak, yi hear me! A need a proper jakit fur this... nane ae yir Peter Storm. A need all-mountain protection!*

Absolute wee patter merchant. Ma maw, pragmatic wuman as ever, asks me... how much is a Berrghis? A always laughed at the way she pronounced it. Two hundred and fifty pounds, they wur. She just laughed n started talkin aboot plastic ponchos n aw this. A'm like, *Maw, A'm an Airdrie boy, no Pocahontas!* We're drivin back fae the toon n A spy an outdoor shop n it says OUTDOOR WORLD – BIG DISCOUNTS! A'm pointin oot the passenger windae, *MAW! Outdoor gear on the cheap, mone!* Ma maw rolls the brief aff the motorway n we bounce intae the discount warehouse. There it is. The holy grail. Two hundred and twenty-five pounds fur a blue Mera Peak. Ma maw remains dubious aboot the price, obviously blissfully unawares ae the profound cultural significance ae such a jakit. It wis pure gang fashion in the early 2000s. Cos A'm going tae the BB camp on Arran she agrees n gits me it. Buzzin wisnae even the word.

The day comes n everybody is in the wee hut in Corrie gittin geared up n ready tae smash aw 2,867 feet ae Goatfell. It's a meaty wee Corbett. We wur headed up the front, then we wur marchin along the Saddle ridge, droppin down intae Glen Sannox via the wee dodgy rocky chimney at the back, beneath the mighty pyramid ae Cìr Mhòr, then haufin it back tae the waitin minibus fur exfiltration. Wan ae the leaders remarked at the Berghaus jakit. 'That's a cracking bit of kit, Graeme!' A just laughed n replied *A'm no wearin that, yi mad?!* The hallowed Mera Peak wis too precious tae be rollin aboot hills wae it, gittin it aw filthy n that. A pulled on a cotton Air Max hoody n a Rangers scarf n headed oot the door, only tae be absolutely soakin n freezin later. Wit a fat trek it wis. We got tae the tap ae the Saddle, which is, by any stretch ae the imagination, an alpine environment wae dramatic rocky faces n deep glens on either side. A pair ae eagles fly through the air, callin tae each other n A swear tae God, A didnae know the world could be that beautiful. Or, in fact, A did, but A hud kinda forgot. We completed the mish n got back in wan piece n the next week A quit the BBs. That Friday night, A hud ma Mera Peak on fur real n we aw stood in the woods in the dark n the wet drinkin Buckfast n smokin fags n ma mind went tae the trip n the lads back in the hall. Maybe thinkin choices ir conditioned by moral deities is a mystic world view. A find it hard tae fathom they irnae, when yi think ae where the snakin paths lead. A swallow the feelin, but it goes doon bitter.

Sixteen years later, A bang intae wan ae the officers. A tell him A never forgot the Arran trip n leavin wis wan ae ma biggest regrets. Later that night, he sends me the pictures fae the camp that A hud never seen. A look so young n daft in them. People would say constant, yi just got in wae the wrong crowd or yi took the wrong road, son. Others say everyhin happens fur a reason. They say there ir nae wrong roads, predestination n aw that. This wisnae the hero's journey. This wis the bad path wae the anti-heroes. A wis wan ae them. Eventually, we would gie the lads walkin past us in their smart uniforms a hard time n bam them up fur no runnin aboot wae the troops. A imagine an alternative scenario where A hud walked past maself n intae that hall, rather than standin doon they dark wids, drinkin wine in the pissin rain. Things might huv been different. Grin n bear it, cos they wurnae. It's this place tae blame, some people say. Wis it a series ae complex sociological n cultural phenomena n personal circumstances resultin in aw that madness or wis it destiny? Ir we convinced every detail ae oor lives ir continually woven together fur good? Dae yi believe in resurrection... or only in Russian trance? Some say walkin, talkin sea monkeys huv delusions ae grandeur in faith. Heaven knows Airdrie is wan hell ae a toon. Best people yeel meet. Night's darkness dissolves away. The searcher ae the heart knows fully oor longings.

Share your love of books. . .

Scottish Book Trust is an independent national charity. Our mission is to ensure people living in Scotland have equal access to books.

If you're enjoying this book, please consider making a donation so that everyone in Scotland has the opportunity to improve their life chances through books and the fundamental skills of reading and writing.

Visit **scottishbooktrust.com/donate** to find out more.

Finding my place

A Ceilidh Through Time
Jacqueline Munro

I'm spinning and laughing and sweating; it is joy and it is life.

The soaring song of the fiddle thrums in my bones, every breath of the accordion as essential as my own; the tapping of feet and rapping of drums is the echo of my heartbeat as I dance and dance and dance.

Here, time has no bearing. It's just us, the room, the music and all the ones who came before, connected through a shared moment of culture and jubilance. A long tradition of gathering to share stories and songs that whisper to us now – listen...

Can you hear it? Can you feel it?

Can you hear their sorrow and pain in the lilting singing? Their strength and endurance in the pounding of feet and drums? Can you feel their soul and merriment in the clasp of hands and tangle of limbs?

Every song, every step is a story that I share with the one I love, my family, my friends and complete strangers as we kick and clap and spin. The band spill their very souls into the instruments, pouring the music into our own, a conduit for communication spanning hundreds of years so that nothing will ever be forgotten.

And with our panting breaths and pulsing blood, we keep the stories alive.

A young couple married and full of purest love celebrating with their clan, an enduring light to fight back any darkness. The gathering of families in farewell of their children going off to war, so that they may take this moment with them and think of home. Faerie folk with the grass under their feet tickling their toes, yielding themselves entirely to the magic of the forest and the earth.

'Live,' the music demands. 'Live and dance and remember.'

The cascading notes peel back the worries, the insecurity, the nonsense until nothing exists beyond this moment. Just your hand in theirs and the swirling of the dance, as sure and beautiful as the rippling stars in the night sky.

It doesn't matter where you hail from, it doesn't matter that you trip over your feet, that your face is flushed and hair damped with sweat. To dance here is to be free. When you take a stranger's sweat-slick palm and throw each other around, grinning wildly. Or stumble as you weave in and out of bodies, laughing with abandon. Your happiness is theirs, and theirs is yours.

With song and dance, we tell the stories of love and loss and home. We're reminded that all that exists is love and each other. We squeeze a little bit tighter, hold on a little longer and feel a little bit more. As if every person to revel in the music before or sit around the storyteller left a piece of themselves for you, and you'll leave a piece of yourself for everyone after.

The music fills me up with all those lives and stories, the floating strings and rolling keys swelling my heart, and I give myself over to it. I promise not to forget the feeling, the joy and the clarity, of existing wholly in this moment.

And when the song comes to its crashing end and I'm released from its thrall, collapsing with heavy breaths and a beaming smile, my bursting heart thuds and every beat says: 'I am home, I am home, I am home.'

Author note: *This was inspired by attending a few rescheduled weddings and the feeling of getting to dance with people again. I've lived in Scotland for nine years now and been to my fair share of ceilidhs, and I love them. There's something about them that always makes time seem to stop.*

Here
Fiona Stuart

I like to stay up all night and sleep all day. Remember that, before the kids came? Like last Christmas when we binge-watched Netflix, just us. Then we went to Portobello beach. 'No porto, no bello' my godmother used to say, amused (she visited many fine ports in her life), but in a way I think it is both beautiful and a port of a sort.

On New Year's Day Porty beach reminds me of a Victorian holiday. Swimmers brave the ocean spray and we promenade side by side – timeless and we don't need to say much. It's a pleasure and a sanctuary – a tonic.

When we first came to Edinburgh, I felt sure that craggy old Arthur's Seat would be my beau, but we lived in Leith and my job was in Portobello at a recording studio with rehearsal rooms. I cycled every day, rain and shine, against and with the forces pushing from the north. No matter what was going on with us, with life, with work, Portobello beach had the ability to hold me up and bring me beyond myself.

The studio, based in an old Scottish Power archive building (where reams of paper data had been stored and catalogued) was always on borrowed time and was eventually washed away by the high tide of development. The aisles of Aldi now stand where once women and men strummed and sang and beat their drums. The iron windows used to rattle in the briny evening air, reminiscent of the typewriters that tapped before them. The seagulls all line up, proud along the roof as they always were, and I continue to visit the beach.

Staying up all night is for the young, who spark like plankton in the dark. Life moves on. We had a family but I never took to being a mum the way I assumed I would. Nothing prepared me for my crying child. The pressure – like the ocean abyss – is a mad midnight zone for me, but Portobello beach is accessible and the whingeing stops. They are happy, and I can *be*. Children busily fetch water, dig sand, collect treasure… I sit without anyone demanding of me, like a gull resting on the water, just bobbing there on the surface in peace, watching.

The Firth of Forth is sometimes a luminescent window to the sky. Other days it is restless and turbulent or wild and expressive, spitting into the wind. It is ecstasy. It is melancholy. Mostly though, it is plain. The waves lap, unimaginative – disappointed. Their energy has gone. It has dissipated into the profound body of water. The sea and the beach become one.

Working nine to five it can be hard to keep real dreams alive and we find ourselves drifting like flotsam. I forget, but we live with the undertow of mental illness. It is threatening and is hard on us all, and some of the positives in our lives have been jettisoned over time to keep us afloat. Even now, in good health, there are issues that wrap around us like the rubbish left behind on the prom after a perfect day. It can be a storm and the kind of darkness that goes on and on but I'm a lighthouse and this dirty beach is a desert island. We don't hit the rocks. The beach is littered, the sea is brown, the mountains are bleak but it is strangely beautiful and, directionless, the seabirds fly over. Here, I can dream.

It's a summer's day. It is like a Victorian holiday, only we beachcomb and find plastic instead of bone. I'm dreaming of being in a little boat. I row out away from the people to be like the seabirds that fly, directionless over Portobello beach.

The tide has turned and my youth is retreating slowly towards the wide horizon. My memories are like lugworms; clueless, popping up on the silt flats that sparkle in the winter light. I keep my own snapshot archives of pure happiness and this city beach is ever-present: I eat chips with my toddler – cheeks ruddy from the cold; I swim with my belly as full with baby as it could be, the day before he was born; we glue our teeth together with home-made treacle toffee as we watch fireworks on bonfire night; we clink plastic flutes at sunset; my little girl draws lines in the sand that disappear like magic and the low sun shimmers across her; we eat ice cream in the wind; we eat oysters – handsome in the rain; we scuttle over rocks like crabs, looking for life; the light is dull and my two children – crouched down – are beaming.

I like to stay up all night and sleep all day, but it's rarely a good idea. We're leaving the city now, to seek space to grow with our young family. We won't be as near to the beach. Without this desert island as a neighbour, I wonder where my next harbour will be. Which place will serve to remind me that heaven is *here*?

Author note: *I've been thinking about 'place' a lot recently as we uprooted and moved out of the city, leaving all our safe havens behind. Our new home is surrounded by inspiring nature that makes me want to write. When I used to cycle along Portobello prom to work every day, it occurred to me that the beach was like a desert island – a place I felt peaceful and cut off from everything else going on.*

Clachnaben
Jane Swanson

Some hills I have climbed only once. Some hills I have returned to again and again. Some hills have helped me find peace and new perspectives when life has been challenging. Clachnaben in Glen Dye in Aberdeenshire is one such hill. A familiar landmark on Lower Deeside, Clachnaben is topped with a large granite tor, a rocky outcrop that rises abruptly from the slope of the hill, and from a distance looks like a ruined fortress. The name Clachnaben comes from the Gaelic 'Clach na Beinne' meaning the Stone on the Hill.

It is an overcast day in August, and after a recent bereavement I am once again drawn to Clachnaben. I park in the old quarry north of the Bridge of Dye and follow the wide path through the woods. The trees are a mix of ancient Scots pines, Douglas firs and larches. Beneath them are willowy ferns and blaeberry bushes with small, glossy leaves and dark purple berries. The trees are hushed, and my feet make no sound on a soft carpet of rust-coloured pine needles. The air is warm and still, fresh with the peppery, minty scent of pine, which invites me to breathe… slowly… and deeply. And this is where the magic starts; the simple rhythm of walking, of lifting and setting down each foot in turn gently unknots the tension in my mind.

I follow the track to the bottom of the glen, cross the bridge over the river and fork right towards an expanse of open country known as Miller's Bog. The broad swathe of heath and pasture grazed by sheep welcomes me back like a long-lost friend with wide, outstretched arms. The space, stillness and silence invite me to reflect and reframe the difficult experience of the past few months.

The granite tor of Clachnaben lies ahead, inky blue against the grey sky, shaped like a molar tooth with jagged, pointed cusps. In local folklore, the tor is sometimes called 'The Devil's Bite'. The story goes that the devil took a bite out of the hillside but it tasted sour, so he spat it out over the top of Clachnaben and this is the origin of the tor. Other stories tell of giants hurling rocks at each other, and that the tor is a boulder hurled across the hills by Jock O' Bennachie at his rival Jock O' North, who lived on the Tap O' North close to Rhynie.

I think about the anger Jock must have felt as he lifted the boulder, and as I picture him hurling it across the hills, something of my anguish travels alongside the enormous piece of granite. I picture the boulder crashing down onto Clachnaben with a thundering thud, the ground quaking, the rock shattering and clouds of dust rising into the sky. Eventually the dust and the giants' anger would have settled, and in the moment, my anguish is stilled.

I stroll along the path and over the wooden footbridge; the ambling pace of my feet mirrors the slow, lilting rhythm of the river and for the first time in a long while I sense an ease of being in my body and in my mind. Ahead the path meanders uphill though a plantation of straggly windswept pines with low-sweeping branches and feathery, fey, light green pine needles. The path keeps to the edge of the trees and follows the fast-flowing Mill Burn. My mind drifts between the different sensory experiences; the lively musicality of the water, the gentle rustle of the trees and the sight of the thick, lush grass on the banks of the burn. It is impossible not to feel enlivened and optimistic.

At the top of the plantation the path cuts left across the pink and purple heather and follows the col between Clachnaben and Mount Shade. The air vibrates with the buzz of hundreds of bees hovering in and out of the tiny bell-shaped flowers. I brush my hands over the springy, wiry heather; it has a sweet scent, woody, mossy, like the smell of a hay-filled barn on a warm summer's day.

The narrow path follows the shoulder of the hill to ease the ascent and is well-built with neat pink granite steps. Even so it is a strenuous climb: my leg muscles burn, my heart beats faster and the lumbering sound of my breath thumps in my ears. The path broadens out and cuts up to the left. It's stony and sandy underfoot, the tor looms above me with the majesty and mystery of an enchanted castle. The granite is elephant-grey in colour, in places the vertical folds and crevices in the rocks remind me of an elephant's rugged, wrinkled hide. The path heads round to the right, to the back of the tor, which is easier to climb. I scramble to the top and sit down. It feels like being on top of the world.

The ridge of Bennachie lies to the north with the rounded summit of Oxen Craig and the conical peak of Mither Tap; in the distance there are patches of snow on Lochnagar, and to the east is the grey North Sea. The tower blocks beside Aberdeen beach look like tiny, upended Lego bricks. I feel rejuvenated, at peace with myself and the world, and energised to face the future. Clachnaben never fails me.

Sunday. . . (Black and White)

Des Mcanulty

I am back.

McChuills.

I used to come here. Sunday. When I felt all yingy and
yangy and yucky. After a night in the Suby. Or the Arches
or the Art School. I was with those of ilk. A communal
lapse of Catholicism. All seeking forgiveness for sins
from nights prior. Imagined or otherwise. If only we
knew how much one hour from our week in the Chapel
would soothe our wee mammies' hearts. But it's here
we seek penance. Black, black, black and then white.
We glugged that drink back with our eyes closed. And
when they open. Forgiveness. Rationale. No need for
penance. The music is soulful and whole. You can see
in your mind the dancing that once accompanied these
old songs. In a dance hall down the road. Love was
found here. Most sparked brightly then soured. Some
blossomed and flew. Children run the Glasgow streets.
Born from love that began over cold pints in these
corners. Mates and colleagues. Lunchtime to kicking-
oot time. Brothers and sisters, diary dates met. Fathers'
first pints with sons. Son's last pint with fathers. In here.
It all happened in here. And now I am back. Back here
with my son. He wants my phone and cares little for
the emotional pull this place has on me. He'll come here
with his own friends one day. At least, I hope he does.
I stay for a while longer. An older man than I'd ever

thought I'd be. The black and white falls with the same glorious ease. I wish it was a long-gone Sunday, but those times aren't coming back. As I leave, I notice two old ace faces. Keeping the place sharp. If they remain, so too will the memories. Whatever the game, whatever the song, as the dance goes on, down the old years. I hope I am always welcome here.

Author note: *I took my nine-year-old son Elliott for lunch into McChuills, a famous pub on High Street, Glasgow. This was a pub my friends and I would frequent in our twenties. We would go there on a Sunday for Guinness to cure our hangovers and hang-ups. It's still a great pub.*

Let the Shadows Fall
Helen Fields

California. We were living the dream. Sunset walks on the beach, lazy weekends by the grill, chatting with neighbours, sunshine on tap. My husband, children and I had left our extended family behind in England and flown off to live in the USA. And then disaster struck. The details don't matter, but my reaction to it does. For the first time in my life, I was dealing with stress that was just too much for me. Emotions that were too raw to face. A crisis that threatened to unravel me completely.

In the midst of it all, I had a trip planned to Scotland. That wasn't unusual. My books are set in Scotland, it's a country I love and know well, and whilst living in the US I was doing a fairly regular international commute for events and book tours. On that one occasion, however, it felt like the last thing I needed.

I set off from Los Angeles heavy-hearted, feeling sick to my stomach. The flight seemed to last forever, transferring at Heathrow and finally landing in Edinburgh. I went straight to a hotel, and took to bed. Twelve hours of sleep and one hot shower later, I dragged my sorry self to the car hire company and picked up my ride for the next week, so jet-lagged that I stuck a post-it note on the dashboard proclaiming in large red letters, 'DRIVE ON LEFT!'. Then I got on the road and headed north.

My purpose was to hit a few bookshops, sign some books, catch up with a few people I knew along the way, but mostly to check out locations for my next two books.

I'd packed badly for the transition between the burning heat of Southern California and the less tropical climes of Scotland – by which I mean I'd neglected to even pack a coat, and my warmest item was an old hoodie. And so I began to drive, heating blasting, the satnav doing an unimpressive job, wearing my sadness like the scarf I should actually have packed.

I stopped first in Kinross, where I bought takeaway coffee and a bacon roll, then found a car park overlooking Loch Leven. I cried there for an hour, watching shades of grey dance on the water's glassy surface, listening to the silence. Other cars came and went. Dog walkers passed me and raised a greeting hand. A bird, hoping for scraps, watched me from a post. We shared the bacon roll, little by little, as I sat on the bonnet of the car and let the wind dry the tears from my face. I breathed Scotland's air. I looked across the water to the island where the ruins of Lochleven Castle sat, and I tried to recall the tidbits I knew of its history. I was fairly certain that Robert the Bruce had visited there once. More sure that Mary Queen of Scots had stayed there as a guest, later imprisoned there and forced to abdicate.

I lost time, fingers curled around my slowly cooling coffee, imagining the comings and goings across Loch Leven. The endless sun-up-sun-down of that churning, bloody history. By the time my imagination was exhausted, even the bird had given up waiting for more food. I began driving again, this time heading for Braemar.

The sun shone a little that afternoon as I went. Not enough to heat the air, but sufficient to put shadows at the sides of trees and at the edge of the growing hills. It wasn't the Californian sun and I was grateful for that. It didn't suck the oxygen from your lungs, and threaten burns from too long an exposure. It was a herd of deer that stopped me in my tracks, made me pull over to watch them run, leap, eat, run, leap, eat, along the foothills of the glorious Cairngorms. I stood at the side of the road, not another car in sight, and I basked in it. The Cairngorm region has a light I've found nowhere else on Earth. Always tinted slightly blue, come winter or summer. It's a clean light, a true light. In that moment I was reminded of a Walt Whitman quote:

'Keep your face turned always towards the sun, and the shadows will fall behind you.'

Metaphor or not, I did just that. I turned into the sunshine, closed my eyes, and I let myself be thankful for those seconds. For the vastness of the place I was in. For the nature surrounding me. And I drove once more.

In Braemar that night, I didn't hide in my room. I found a pub serving food, I sat at the bar, and I talked to the woman serving the drinks. We talked about nothing much, as only the Scots can. We laughed for no particular reason, which is what the Scots are good at. And when I was done, the woman who'd kept me company put her hand on mine, looked me in the eyes, and said, 'You're all right, sweetheart. Everything's going to be all right.'

I don't think I'd told her that I was troubled. I certainly didn't impart any of the details of the crisis we were in at home. She just knew, and was able to reach out with flesh and bone and touch my hand, and it didn't solve anything or change anything, but it was everything to me.

I didn't cry again for the rest of that journey. I wasn't happy, I don't think, but the weight was gone. As I drove, and visited, and took in the scenery that can only be Scotland, something changed.

It wasn't until I was back on a plane, looking down as we took off, that I realised how Scotland had healed me. It's all about scale. The sense of being one tiny part of a much bigger thing. When you stand by a loch, or on a mountain side, or in the highlands, or on a beach in Scotland, there is peace. There is peace because nature has been preserved there, protected, loved. Nature is at the top of the agenda. Which means you, as a visitor, can find your proper place within it.

But the scale of Scotland is about history too. It's about realising that the world will keep turning. You can fight your battles, win or lose. You can choose sides and go screaming into the fight. But a next day will come, and the night after that. And all the things you fought for or railed against will change once more.

Scotland had always been, I now understand, my temple. That visit simply gave me pause to think about why. It's where I go to plug myself in, to recharge in all the ways that matter. Scotland is my therapy. My food and drink.

I returned home able to face the world, and better able to help others heal. All it took was to stop and breathe a while, and to remember how temporary everything is.

Tales to treasure

Foxes
Iris Potter

My dad came across an abandoned fox cub when he was of primary school age. He cared for and looked after it but when it got older it was crying each night to be let out. It was causing a lot of disturbance and much annoyance to the neighbours. So rather reluctantly he had to let it go. Thankfully though, the fox still visited my dad.

He was really happy when he came across a fox's den near our house. That was fourteen years ago and it turned out that six cubs were born there. My dad started feeding them so since then we have had them at our door every night.

We are now at the great-grandchild stage and it's been an absolute joy having them all here. They bring so much joy and happiness. They are all named and they know their names too.

There was a time in 2008 a few days before bonfire night when there were loads of random fireworks getting thrown about and the noise was frightening. That was the first night ever that the foxes didn't turn up. This went on for three nights in a row. We were so upset and thought that they'd been spooked and moved off to live somewhere else and we wouldn't see them again.

It was midnight and we were all heading to bed and the security light went on. We ran to the door and we were so happy to see one of our foxes, Sophie. We got her some food and she kept walking away from us. We followed her and she took us to the side of the house where our wheelie bin was up in flames, right beside our gas box.

It turned out someone had put lit fireworks inside our bin!

When we spoke with the fireman they said if we weren't alerted to that fire we would've certainly come to harm. So we believe Sophie saved our lives.

There have also been funny incidents with them too.

One morning, around 1am, two foxes were having a bit of a barney. My sister, who was in her nightdress and slippers, decided that she was going out to intervene. When she came back out of the bushes the police were driving by and, as we stay across the road from a care home, they stopped, thinking that she'd escaped. They didn't believe her when she said, 'I stay in that house over there. I'm just out here to stop my foxes fighting!'

But that didn't help and they led her by the arm to the care home door. She pleaded with them and said, 'Please go over to that house and my sister will tell you.'

They came over and I was very tempted to say, 'Oh she does live in the care home and she's always escaping.'

It was so funny, a golden moment.

She's Got the Beat
Paul Foy

Time had come up with all sorts of thingamabobs and whatsits to keep Auntie Maureen occupied, right up to her mid-nineties. Eventually, as was inevitable, it ran out of ideas.

My nine-year-old twin daughters, Sarah and Faith, couldn't remember a time when they hadn't known Auntie Maureen with her huge collection of teddy bears, some almost as old as her: they'd been to the charity coffee mornings she helped out with; it had become traditional that she'd come with us to the Forres garden centre for a bowl of Cullen skink. So now, going to visit her in an old people's home was not just sad, it was incomprehensible and frightening.

We were up in Moray for our annual summer stay in Findhorn. The weather was nice, warm enough for people to sit out in the sandstone building's well-maintained and colourful garden, so why was it deserted like the grounds of the castle in *Beauty and the Beast*? The sky was clear, yet a cold chill seemed to pass through us as though a large black bird had covered the sun.

The lady at reception assured us that Auntie Maureen was settling in nicely and had just finished her lunch, sponge pudding and all. She could get a little bit confused, but, 'You'll know about that. Yes?' She gave the girls a sympathetic smile. 'She can't wait to see you two. Such a fine old lady.'

Faith chewed her lower lip and Sarah held in check

any expression tempted to slip onto her face. We entered a high-ceilinged room with rows of armchairs facing a wall-mounted TV that had the sound turned down. Easy-listening music played through a single speaker high up in one of the corners of the room. My girls' eyes scampered furtively over the old folk slouched into those armchairs, some looking at the silent screen, some fast asleep, some staring at nothing in particular. It must have seemed to the little ones like a dark enchantment had been cast over the place.

Auntie Maureen was in good spirits, sitting with her back to the wall that the TV was mounted onto. She had a round table next to her on which was a plate of biscuits and a jug of juice. She looked well, much brighter than she'd been the last time we'd seen her in her home. She appeared to be completely aware of her current situation, happy enough with it, almost back to her old self. Almost.

'How are you liking it here?' asked Kaitlyn, my wife.

'I'm fine.'

'You've got everything you need?' asked Kaitlyn's sister, Janice.

'Oh yes. I've got my own room, I get three meals a day, and they keep me supplied with biscuits and fruit and all the booze I can drink.'

I disguised a laugh as cough. Sarah and Faith gave me a reprimanding look with the intensity that only small girls can manage.

'Are you sure about that, Maureen?'

'Oh yes. They disguise it as raspberry juice.' She indicated the jug on the table. 'And it's strong stuff. Whoof!'

More general chat followed, about how she was feeling, had she watched anything good on the telly – 'I like that *Pointless* programme, but I never know any of the answers' - that sort of thing.

I left the small talk to Kaitlyn and Janice, so I was first to notice the worried expressions on Faith and Sarah's faces. I looked to where they were looking and saw a wrinkled wee woman in her old lady skirt and blouse walking towards us. I also noticed that an upbeat song, Connie Francis' 'Stupid Cupid', was playing through the speaker.

Faith looked at me, worried, as the old woman stopped silently in front of her. Sarah looked relieved, suddenly alive with interest.

I shrugged my shoulders. How was I meant to know what to do?

The woman smiled and raised her arms directly in front of Faith, palms up. She nodded, indicating that she wanted Faith to put her hands in hers. We were all watching now, though nobody had any advice to offer.

There was nothing else for it. Faith put her hands into those of the old woman, who smiled and began to bend her knees in time to the music, her upper body twisting from side to side as far as her ancient tendons would allow. As they were holding hands, Faith had no choice but to move as well. She looked lost at first, but then she began to bend her knees, shuffling her feet as she upped the tempo of the twisting. The woman's eyes sparkled, and when she let go of one of Faith's hands, my daughter knew exactly what to do. She lifted the joined hands up high and twirled round and under her partner's arm, then twisted back the other way and stepped back, throwing her arm out to the side. The woman did the same with her free arm, though not quite with the grace and ease of movement that Faith had, but it was clear that once upon a time she'd learned how to jive. As she danced now, the shimmering glow from the TV covered her in a wash of movement and colour that seemed to have danced its way from the past into this moment, obliterating the years between her and the girl who complemented her steps and patterns.

The music changed to a slow-tempo song by Perry Como and the woman shrank back into the shape that Time had slowly worked her into. She dropped her arms to her sides, said nothing, and returned to her seat.

When we were leaving she looked and smiled, giving a little wave. Faith paused and smiled back, then followed us out. As we left I was sure I could feel something strange in the atmosphere. I tell myself it was probably just the residue that magic leaves behind.

Author note: *We were visiting my wife's auntie after she'd had to move into an old people's home. My twin daughters were feeling very uneasy, especially when an old lady approached them and without saying anything took one of my daughter's hands and started dancing. At first my daughter didn't know what to do, but then she started dancing too and a little moment of magic happened.*

Cheesie McCraw
Jennie Murray

He cam tae us in the lockdoon,
A dreich, drear March day,
The win snell an scoorin fae the East.
Black-nebbit, black as Auld Nick's soul,
Bit no murderin! Jist a bit craw,
Sair trauchelt, hirplin,
His left leg hauden heich;
A puir thing, jist wantin a chance, a bield.
We gied him meat,
Brose, mince,
Weel awa fae aw the ithers.
We cried him Cheesie,
An he thruive,
Each an evry day a bit mair strang.
An each an evry day, we cry 'Crawlad!'
An whiles, he answers us;
A contact caw, ye micht say!
Oor gairden, his howff,
Oor birch, his ruist.
He trusts us noo,
Waitin on the grass fir his bit meat.
Oan bricht days, wi the sun in the lift
He likes tae strut an preen;
In the dark days, he hunkers doon,
Humphie-backit, his puir leg grievin him sair.
An we think he's a bit like us,
Sair trauchelt, hirplin,
Ae day blythe,

Ae day dulesome an dowie;
An we preen oor feathers,
An we thole the pain.
We howp fir a ruist, an luve, an trust,
We caw awa, wi a wee bit meat;
An howp that, ae day, we'll aw flee,
Free.

Author note: *Lots of birds come to our garden. Cheesie was instantly identifiable, because of his limp. (We are still not sure if he is male or female!) Now, two years later, he is still with us, along with his mate, and with four young Cheesies!*

The Quilted Dressing Gown
Hannah McDonald

Francis Murphy was my best pal. He lived across the
road from me, in a four-in-a-block exactly like ours,
a mirror image of our own home. When I was young
I thought the biggest difference between us was the
number of people who lived in our houses – there was
me, my mammy and daddy, and my big brother John
in our house. In his house there was him, his mammy
and daddy, and his eight siblings. This reflected a bigger
difference between us, a thing that sometimes felt like
nothing and other times was everything; Francis and his
family were Catholic, and me and my family were not.
On Sundays they went to the village chapel, with the
statues of Mary and Jesus on the walls and the incense
burning and the pageantry of the priest and the altar
boys. We went to the little church at the top of the hill
that had been built by the hands of my grandfather and
his brothers. I would sit in that plain little room, wooden
panels on the walls and threadbare carpets under my
feet, trying not to fall asleep. I would think about Francis
in his chapel, intrigued by the mystery and the rituals I
wasn't allowed to see for myself.

One evening I went into the living room and asked
my mammy if I could go with Francis to the chapel one
Sunday.

'No,' she said, not even looking up from mending one
of John's socks. 'We've got our own church to go to.'

'But I just wanty see what it's like,' I said, in a tone I
hoped would convince her. My daddy was sitting by the

fireplace, eating an orange and throwing the peels into the fire. The room was warm with the smell of citrus. My mammy shook her head.

'No.'

I went in a huff at being told no and didn't speak to anyone until the next morning. When we were eating our porridge, I tried one more time.

'Please Mammy, please let me go to the chapel.' She turned from the sink and looked at me, her eyes burning.

'I'll not tell ye again. You're not going.'

That day I took my time walking home from school. It was late June, warm but with a cloudy sky; I wandered around until I found myself outside the chapel. I looked at the statue of Mary at the front of the building, all white marble and gentle eyes and hands pressed together in supplication. I didn't understand what was so bad about making statues. When I looked at Francis and myself, I couldn't see any difference other than the fact that his fingernails were a bit dirtier than mine. I sat in front of Mary for a while, wondering if she'd somehow give me the answers, but nothing happened. I got up and went home when I stopped being able to feel my hands.

When I got in my mammy was waiting for me in the living room.

'C'mon in,' she said. 'I need to talk to you about something.'

I went in and sat down beside her on the couch. The fire was on; I had seen the pit bus dropping the miners off on my walk back and knew my daddy was due home any minute.

'Tell me,' she said, 'what it was you wanted again for your birthday.' My birthday was two weeks away. I smiled even thinking about it, the one thing I had asked for, the only thing I wanted.

'A quilted dressing gown.' She nodded, and there was sadness in her eyes. She reached into the pocket of her pinny and brought out a neat little bundle of notes.

'Now I think you've been a really good lassie this year, and you deserve to get what you want for your birthday. But Mrs Murphy came to see me; she was awfy upset. She told me that Mr Murphy's been ill and hasn't been able to go to work. They're short on money this month and she's running out of food for the weans.' She paused and looked at me. I knew she was studying my face for a reaction.

'Aye, she does have a lot of mouths to feed.' She nodded.

'Well, she asked me for some money to help her feed them. And I had a look in the money box, but all I had was this money I had set aside for your birthday present. I told Mrs Murphy that I would need to speak to you before I gave her the money, because if I give her the money...' she put her hand on my leg, squeezing it gently. 'It means I won't be able to afford to get you a quilted dressing gown for your birthday.'

Looking back on it now, I know my mammy knew exactly what she was doing. She knew I would never choose a present for myself over my friend and his family having food to eat. And she knew exactly what I would do.

'Well Mammy, obviously I wouldn't want Mrs Murphy to not be able to feed her weans. I think you should give her the money.' She smiled and put her arm around me, pulling me towards her. I let her hug me, breathing in her smell as a few tears escaped from my eyes.

'It's alright to be sad hen, but you did the right thing.'

All that day I felt down about not getting my quilted dressing gown. But then I thought about my mammy and her kindness – the way she wanted to help Mrs Murphy, how she'd asked me before she did it even though she knew I'd never say no, the fact that it didn't matter to her that she and Mrs Murphy went to different churches. When it came down to it, it was a neighbour helping a neighbour. I knew that must be something that got taught in all churches.

Faeries
Jamie Aitken

'We're going to see if we can see any faeries!'

At the ripe old age of eight years old, I already had
a healthy level of cynicism around this idea when my
mum suggested it one summer. However, I still felt a
tingle of excitement flutter in my stomach.

We were on the way to Calderglen Country Park in the
vast wilderness of East Kilbride, myself, my cousin and
my little brother strapped into the back of my auntie's
Volkswagen Polo. I remember the overstretched elastic
holding the multicoloured seat covers on the seats, the
sweet, rancid smell of old cigarettes and my brother
and cousin constantly elbowing one another in the ribs.
Tears came, inevitably, but my memory hasn't retained
which of them it was.

We bundled out of the car and were greeted by the
familiar cacophony of sounds that only a car park
in East Kilbride on a sunny day during the summer
holidays could produce. We stood against the car, caked
in a layer of sun cream. I'm pretty sure we all ended up
burnt anyway.

After the joy that only seeing a huge, stinking pig
rolling about in its own jobbie can bring to three young
children, we took our lunch to the big open area where
there were trees the likes of which I have seen no equal
to since. My mum and auntie watched nervously as we
three challenged each other to climb higher and higher.
Afterwards, we wolfed down our lukewarm sandwiches,
ravenous after a day already filled with adventure.

That was when my mum made her announcement. She said it with such enthusiasm and the younger ones got so excited, I couldn't help but get swept up in the charade. I gave my mum a knowing look and she winked at me and smiled.

We wandered into the woodlands then, keeping our eyes out for the telltale signs of faerie inhabitancy: gnarly trees with interesting knots, clusters of mushrooms (that you had better not touch!), fallen trees with roots reaching out like a witch's beckoning fingers and of course tiny little footprints.

'Thanks for taking us here, good to get away from the hospital for a bit.'

'Ach away and don't be daft, you don't need to say thanks.'

I was walking just behind my mum and auntie, double-checking behind the line of ferns that there weren't any mushrooms hiding in there.

'I know, but it really is appreciated. The boys were quite upset. They still don't really understand what's happening, although I think Jamie's starting to cop on that this is pretty serious,' my mum said in a voice that sounded ready to crack.

'He's no as daft as he looks. He knows his daddy's no well, I heard him telling his brother.'

My auntie lit a cigarette and passed it to my mum, who accepted it gratefully.

'Aye, but how "no well" really? I mean none of us know that. But the look on the doctors' faces this morning. I'm really starting to think he might not...'

'Listen, we don't need to dwell on that. He's a fighter and he's got these two boys and you to fight for.'

I did understand it was bad with my dad. I hadn't seen him in what felt like months but it was more like a couple of weeks, if that. He had been fine, and then he wasn't. He was in a hospital in Edinburgh and we weren't allowed to see him yet, my brother and me. All we knew was that he was a very strange yellow colour, had lots of tubes sticking in him and he couldn't talk as there was a pipe helping him breathe. He had always been so strong, I couldn't imagine him laid up, not able to get up and hug us, or give me a pretend slap around the head. I could feel the warmth in my face start to creep up and knew the tears were coming. That's when I saw it.

In the corner of my eye, just as we reached the water's edge: a sparkle. Not a twinkle or a flash or a reflection, but a sparkle. Up a tree, just to the right of the rushing river and the stepping stones to cross it. I gave a huge shout, causing my mum and auntie to leap out of their skin, and raced to the spot, my brother and cousin hot on my heels. I looked up at the tree, searching every nook and cranny, scratching my legs on the undergrowth as I clambered around to the other side.

'Jamie, away from the edge!' my mum shouted, but I had to find it. It had to be there, it just had to!

I was ready to give up, I could feel my mum getting more angry as I refused to come away from the water. Then, just as I was about to stop, I saw them. Two long, silver, silky wings, fluttering into a crack in the tree, high above me. There was no mistaking what I had seen. A faerie. I had seen my first faerie. I could hardly believe it. My jaw dropped open and I felt a tingle all over my body. I had seen it. I ran back around the tree, soaking my velcro trainers and wrapped my arms tightly around my mum.

'I saw one, Mum, I saw one for sure!'

The next year we visited that same spot. Unfortunately, I didn't see a faerie that day. It was overcast and had rained, and the river was much higher. However, I showed my dad the spot where I had seen my very first faerie. I told him that magic was real, and squeezed his hand tightly. That day was even better than the year before.

Author note: *This is a story about my father recovering from a life-threatening illness, and childhood innocence. It is dedicated to the Scottish Liver Transplant Unit based in Edinburgh, who helped two little boys grow up with their father, and made us all believe in miracles and magic.*

Yellowcraig

Kirsty Niven

Polystyrene hail flings down
while the sun beats and beats,
nonsensically Scottish
and oddly beautiful –
perfectly framed by the square
of the caravan's tin window.
A morse code soundtrack
taps itself out on the roof
as I scribble in my notebook.
Pins and needles in my feet,
trapped under the snoring Clumber,
but at least they're warm.
The pencil grinds down to a nub,
pages overflowing in a gush
with thoughts and plots.
Inspiration and imagination unlocked
by the safety and peace
of a home away from home.

The kettle clicks on, their naps are over,
just as 'the end' is etched in block capitals.

Author note: *This poem is inspired by holidays spent
with my Gran and Great-Gran as a child, where I would
write in the afternoons while they napped.*